THE DEEP TRUTH

THE DEEP TRUTH

A Study of Shelley's Scepticism

C. E. PULOS

UNIVERSITY OF NEBRASKA PRESS · Lincoln · 1962

TO MARIA

WHILE this study attempts a new approach to Shelley's thought through an investigation of his hitherto neglected scepticism, it necessarily recognizes four other traditions as important influences on the poet — political radicalism, empiricism, Platonism, and Christianity. The radical, Platonic, and Christian influences on Shelley are not presented in detail because they are well known and require no fresh demonstration.

A new approach to Shelley's thought seems imperative in view of the so-called contradictions discovered in it by critic after critic. My purpose, accordingly, is not to weigh one philosophic influence against another but to investigate Shelley's intellectual coherence, to seek the principle by which the poet may have reconciled ideas generally associated with antagonistic traditions. I find such a principle in his hitherto neglected scepticism, which forms the logical center of his thought, the point where his empiricism terminates and his idealism begins. In other words, scepticism is important in Shelley not despite but because of what might be called his eclecticism.

C. E. PULOS

Lincoln, Nebraska
April 15, 1954

CONTENTS

THE DEEP TRUTH

I

INTRODUCTION

PERHAPS no major English poet's philosophy is so elusive as Shelley's. Mrs. Shelley refers to the problem in her note to *Prometheus Unbound:* "It was his design to write prose metaphysical essays on the nature of man, which would have served to explain much of what is obscure in his poetry; a few scattered fragments of observations and remarks alone remain."[1] Whatever the case might have been if we had the poet's systematic prose exposition of his philosophy, his metaphysical fragments in their present form only mirror the difficulties encountered in the poetry. These difficulties do not arise from any real obscurity in the style; they arise, one is tempted to say, from its lucidity. A simple illustration will help to clarify this paradox.

In a letter to Horace Smith, dated April 11, 1822, Shelley declared "that the doctrines of the French, and Material Philosophy, are as false as they are pernicious; but still they are better than Christianity, inasmuch as anarchy is better than despotism; for this reason, that the former is for a season, the latter is eternal." But in the same period of his life we find the poet often expressing seemingly orthodox Christian sentiment, as in the following lines of *The Boat on the Serchio* (1821):

> *All rose to do the task He set to each,*
> *Who shaped us to His ends and not our own.* . . .
>
> (11. 30-31)

These two quotations provide us with a statement of Shelley's thought that has three separable parts: a rejection of French materialism, a preference of such materialism to Christianity, and the apparent expression of a Christian point of view. If the language were obscure on any one or more of these three points, the problem of reconciling them would not be so formidable. But the language is quite clear on all three points. In our bewilderment, we may select one of the three elements in the poet's thought and suppress the other two. Selecting his rejection of French materialism, we may conclude that the poet was fundamentally a disciple of Plato and of Berkeley; emphasizing his preference of French materialism to Christianity, we may try to prove that his real masters were Holbach and Godwin; magnifying the importance of his employment of an apparently Christian point of view, we may argue that he was essentially a religious poet whose views became increasingly Christian as he matured.

Each of our three hypothetical conclusions can be and has been defended—and defended on the basis of no little evidence. Consequently, some critics have come to feel that Shelley's thought lacks a unified tendency and is characterized by basic and irreconcilable contradictions. Such a charge is implied in Hoxie Neale Fairchild's view that "Shelley never lost a piece of intellectual baggage which he had at any time collected."[2] Floyd Stovall comments on this common charge as follows: "There is some justice in the allegation that he was not a systematic thinker. Being an enthusiast rather than a critic, he made little effort to reduce multiform ideas and impressions to strict order; if a new opinion seemed good in itself he was inclined to acknowledge it without first ascertaining whether or not it was consistent with others previously avowed."[3] Some critics, as we shall note in the course of this monograph, have discovered alleged contradictions even in particular poems, or have presented alleged evidence of the poet's misunderstanding of particular authors whose doctrines he employed.

These charges against Shelley's intellectual coherence invite a re-examination of his philosophy, for their premises are derived from traditional interpretations of that philosophy. If we accept certain traditional conclusions regarding Shelley's thought, we must accept also the final verdict that that thought is not free from basic confusion. But I do not find this verdict just. In fact, perhaps no impartial critic believes all or even half the charges that have been made against Shelley's intellectual coherence. And if an impartial critic faces those charges in their totality, he might conceivably suspect the essential validity of the entire lot.

It is true, of course, that Shelley was a voracious reader and that he was influenced by a host of dissimilar writers, both of the past and of his own day. But it is unlikely that he failed to adapt whatever material he drew from others to the synthesis of his own thought. In her note to *The Revolt of Islam* Mrs. Shelley remarks that the poet, according to his own testimony, "deliberated at one time whether he should devote himself to poetry or metaphysics." While his interest in speculative thought declined in his later years, Shelley never completely abandoned the idea of a systematic prose exposition of his philosophy. The following paragraph, found among his prose fragments, suggests not only the wide knowledge of the mature poet, but also the synthesis of that knowledge in a theory of the evolution of thought, terminating in perfectibilitarianism:

> An essay on the progressive excellence perceptible in the expressions—of Solomon, Homer, Bion and the Seven Sages, Socrates, Plato, Theodorus, Zeno, Carneades, Aristotle, Epicurus, Pythagoras, Cicero, Tacitus, Jesus Christ, Virgil, Lucan, Seneca, Epictetus, Antoninus . . . Sulpicius, Severus, Mahomet, Manes, The Fathers—Aristo, Tasso, Petrarch, Dante, Abeillard, Thomas Aquinas—The Schoolmen. The reformers. Spinoza, Bayle, Paschal, Locke, Berkeley, Leibnitz, Melbranche, The French Philosophers, Voltaire, Rousseau, the Germans—the Illuminati—Hume. Godwin—State of General Society. Perfectibility. (VII, 72)

The project outlined in this prose fragment can only mean that Shelley reconciled, at least to his own satisfaction, ideas that some of his critics have found—especially in recent years—quite contradictory.

On the subject of inconsistency one cannot but recall the famous words in Emerson's *Self-Reliance:* "A foolish consistency is the hobgoblin of little minds, adored by little statesmen and philosophers and divines. With consistency a great soul has simply nothing to do." As one can hardly question Shelley's possession of a "great soul," one might accept the theory of his inconsistencies, quoting Emerson in the poet's defence. But the inconsistency of which Emerson approved was not real inconsistency, as his next two paragraphs indicate. Such apparent contradictions as he had in mind are not irreconcilable, if one is able to discover that which unites them: "There will be an agreement in whatever variety of actions, so they be each honest and natural in their hour. For of one will, the actions will be harmonious, however unlike they seem. These varieties are lost sight of at a little distance, at a little height of thought. One tendency unites them all."[4] Let us, therefore, consider Shelley from a little distance, from a little height of thought, in hope of discerning the tendency that unites his ideas.

Descartes, the founder of modern philosophy, swept aside all existing beliefs and deduced his system of thought from these premises: "Cogito ergo sum." From this relatively sceptical beginning, however, he was able to arrive at a considerable body of knowledge, including belief in the doctrine of innate ideas. Welcoming the sceptical spirit of Descartes' approach to philosophy, but rejecting much else, Locke refuted the theory of innate ideas, deriving knowledge solely from experience. Among the concepts that Locke was nevertheless able to salvage were the substances called mind and matter. Influenced by the negative sides of Descartes and Locke, but rejecting some of their positive conclusions, Berkeley denied the existence of matter, converting everything to mind. The last of this line of thinkers was Hume: accepting little more than the negative contributions of his predecessors, Hume denied the existence of mind as well as of matter. In other words, each of the great thinkers following Descartes was strongly impressed only by the negative side of his predecessor's philosophy, until a genuine scepticism inevitably triumphed at last.

This scepticism—the result of the development of thought over a period of nearly two centuries—could hardly constitute anything less than the most important intellectual problem of the next age—the age of romanticism. The central tendency of the romantic movement, viewed as an event in the intellectual history of modern man, was that of reorientation in a world of uncertainty and doubt. Underlying the whole romantic movement is the scepticism of Goethe's Faust:

> *Heisse Doktor und Professor gar*
> *Und ziehe schon an die zehen Jahr*
> *Herauf, herab und quer und krumm*
> *Meine Schüler an der Nas herum*
> *Und seh, dass wir nichts wissen können:*
> *Das will mir schier das Herz verbrennen.*[5]

The reorientation occasioned by this scepticism did not follow a single pattern. One major form of it is reflected in the extension of the scientific method to new areas of investigation: men turned, as Hume had done, from metaphysics to history and the social sciences. Another major form of this reorientation appears in what is loosely referred to as the transcendental movement, manifested in philosophy and literature.

While Kant was responsible for the widespread use of the term, transcendentalism may be traced to earlier writers—to the forerunners of the romantic movement. Of these perhaps none was more important than Rousseau, who wrote in a letter of 1758: "la philosophie, n'ayant sur ces matières ni fond ni rive, manquant d'idées primitives et de principes élémentaires, n'est qu'une mer d'incertitudes et de douts, dont le métaphysicien ne se tire jamais. J'ai donc laissé là la raison, et j'ai consulté la nature, c'est-à-dire le sentiment intérieur qui dirige ma croyance, indépendamment de ma raison. . . ."[6] While Rousseau's words recall the fideism of the Renaissance, they really express a new attitude. Rousseau places his primary faith, not in a traditional creed, but in "nature" and an "interior sentiment." He converts fideism into transcendentalism.

Transcendentalism, however, was not to develop into a single undifferentiated movement, either in literature or philosophy. There were almost as many strains of transcendentalism as the individuals who expressed it. For our purposes, however, it will suffice to distinguish three major varieties of the transcendental tendency in romantic literature.

The dominant form of the transcendental tendency—a form that may be called strict transcendentalism—appears in such writers as Wordsworth, Coleridge, Carlyle, Emerson, Thoreau, and Whitman. Some of these men were considerably more respectful of traditional beliefs than were the rest. They differ likewise in their relation to Oriental philosophy. But despite these and other individual differences, they all came under the direct or indirect influence of the Kantian distinction between "pure reason" and the "understanding." Accepting this distinction more or less dogmatically, and adapting it to their own purposes, they all tended toward a certain degree of confidence in their conclusions about ultimate reality. The influence of scepticism upon them is evident in their preference of intuitive to logical thinking; in most cases it is evident also in their disregard for conventional points of view. But the scepticism of this group is confined largely to the function of the "understanding." Because of their faith in "pure reason," they were able to attain a degree of certitude regarding ultimate reality which constitutes dogmatism, thus obscuring their relation to the sceptical dilemma.

A second form of the transcendental tendency—a form better known as romantic irony—appears in a number of continental romanticists and in Byron. Friedrich Schlegel described romantic irony in the following words: "We must be able to rise above our own love; in our thoughts we must be able to destroy what we worship; otherwise, no matter what other capacities we have, we lack a sense of the infinite and of the world."[7] This form of the transcendental tendency, in other words, attempts to reconcile scepticism and idealism

7

through the employment of irony. The influence of scepticism on the romantic ironist is apparent in his detachment from his ideals, which he recognizes as belonging to the world of appearance or illusion. He avoids the dogmatism of the strict transcendentalists, but leaves his idealism open to the charge of insincerity.

The third form of the transcendental tendency has something in common with each of the two varieties mentioned above, though it also differs from each. It exhibits the sincere idealism of the strict transcendentalist, but not his dogmatism; it possessess the sceptical awareness of the ironic transcendentalist, but not his deliberate irony. This third form of the transcendental tendency is essentially free from the influence of German thought. Its fundamental relation is with the sceptical tradition, whence it derives not only its scepticism but also its "sceptical solution to doubt." This third form of the transcendental tendency is expressed in some measure by Keats,[8] though not in its full scope. It is my hypothesis that Shelley represents this third form of the transcendental tendency and that the fundamental consistency of his thought will emerge if we give sufficient consideration to his relation to the sceptical tradition.

Isolated instances of scepticism in Shelley's poetry and prose have often been noted by the poet's critics. But what renders scepticism important in Shelley is its relation to his thought as a whole: its relation to his rejection of materialism, its relation to his acceptance of Plato, its relation to his attitude toward Christianity. I propose here to deal with these neglected questions. But first it is necessary to present a sketch of the sceptical tradition and to re-examine an obscure and now unrecognized sceptic of Shelley's own time, who is known to have had considerable influence on the poet, but whose thought Shelley's critics have for the most part misinterpreted.

II

THE SCEPTICAL TRADITION

THE sceptical tradition has a long history; and, as one might expect under the circumstances, it exhibits a wide variety of manifestations. But one may roughly divide its history into four periods: the school of Pyrrho, the New Academy, Renaissance scepticism, and Humean scepticism. However unlike one another these four phases of scepticism may be, they all reflect the spirit of doubt, and they all recommend the holding of opinions on the basis of some principle compatible with doubt. The sceptical tradition, then, expresses doubt and seeks a "sceptical solution to doubt."

True scepticism did not appear in Greek thought until toward the end of the fourth century before Christ. A number of remarks in the older philosophy, however, seemed to anticipate the sceptical attitude, enabling the later sceptics, if they so desired, to trace their intellectual lineage to Socratic and even to pre-Socratic philosophy. The words of Democritus that "truth is sunk in an abyss," the confession of Socrates that he knew nothing but the fact of his own ignorance, these and similar assertions by the earlier philosophers were to become a part of the sceptical tradition. There is, however, an important difference between such early expressions of doubt and genuine scepticism. The earlier philosophers were dubitative only with respect to sense knowledge. By developing epistemological theories that did not rest on sensation, they obviated scepticism despite their distrust of the senses. In fact, the more unreliable sense knowledge appeared to be, the more inclined were they to recommend the use of reason. But the sceptics agreed with their contemporaries in regarding the nature of sensation as the only basis of any possible epistemology.[1] They could not distrust sense knowledge, therefore, without distrusting rational knowledge as well.

The emergence of true scepticism in Greek thought coincides with the expansion of the Greek consciousness in the wake of Alexander's conquests. Pyrrho of Elis, the founder of the first school of scepticism, had accompanied Anaxarchus, a philosopher traveling with Alexander's army, as far as India. It was this experience, according to Diogenes Laertius, that led Pyrrho "to adopt a most noble philosophy" (ix. 61).[2] Observing how different peoples disagreed in matters of custom and opinion, he concluded that men's knowledge is confined to their impressions, and that life is governed not by rational principles but by conventions and instincts. Like his contemporaries, Pyrrho was interested mainly in ethics, in the attainment of that repose of mind currently regarded as the highest good. It was to this end, therefore, that he now applied his new awareness of the limitations of reason. Since nothing can be known for certain, the wise man, according to Pyrrho, will cultivate a suspension of judgment in theory, and in practice conform to the existing mores of his country. In this fashion he will attain that tranquility of spirit which is the highest good.

Though Pyrrho left no written works, his doctrines were perpetuated by his pupil, Timon of Phlius. Through Arcesilaus, with whom he was personally acquainted, Timon influenced the school of Plato. The Old Academy, as Plato's original school was henceforth called, had long since declined under the leadership of mediocre men. Meanwhile the Stoics and the Epicureans had come into vogue, and, unmindful of weaknesses in the foundations of their systems, had acquired a confidence rather alien to the best that had been thought and said by the Greek mind. It was this current dogmatism in philosophy that provoked Arcesilaus to convert Plato's school into a school of scepticism, henceforth called the New Academy. The New Academy was to become far more influential than the short-lived school of Pyrrho. Carneades, the fourth head of the New Academy, developed its doctrines more fully and perfected its dialectical method. Though Carneades left no written works, his Carthaginian pupil, Cleitomachus, the fifth head of the New Academy, expounded his master's doctrines in four hundred treatises.

The New Academy differed from the short-lived school of Pyrrho in two important respects. One of these was a difference in method. Conerned primarily with the refutation of philosophical dogmas currently in vogue, the New Academy developed an eristic tendency foreign to Pyrrho. Arcesilaus, according to Diogenes Laertius, was "the first to suspend his judgment owing to the contradictions of opposing arguments. He was also the first to argue on both sides of a question" (iv. 28). A favorite practice of the New Academy was to assume the truth of a current dogma and then to draw logical inferences from it that were either contradictory or otherwise absurd. Aside from method, however, the negative sides of the Academics and the Pyrrhonists exhibit no essential difference. Both in effect demonstrated the impossibility of certitude and advocated the withholding of assent.

The second major difference between the New Academy and the school of Pyrrho belongs to the positive sides of their scepticism. Pyrrho apparently did not develop the positive side of his scepticism to any appreciable degree, so that his philosophy seemed to deprive men of their motives for action and to inculcate an attitude of indifference. The New Academy, on the other hand, developed a theory of probability by which to combat such criticism. According to this theory, while nothing is certain, a good deal is probable; and probability is a sufficient guide in the exercise of human conduct. While the Pyrrhonist, therefore, neither shunned nor pursued anything eagerly, the Academic sceptic was free, as Sextus Empiricus pointed out,[3] to shun the improbable and to pursue the probable with as much intensity as he desired.

In the first century before Christ, Philo of Larissa, the last important Greek exponent of Academic scepticism, began to lay too much stress upon the theory of probability and to maintain that the New Academy was essentially a continuation of the Old. His pupil, Antiochus, took the final step in the dissolution of Academic scepticism: maintaining that the New Academy was a radical deviation from the Old, he deserted Philo and became thoroughly eclectic and dogmatic. But even as it was dying, the New Academy won a champion in the greatest of Roman orators, who tried in vain to revive it.

Cicero was not an original thinker but an interpreter of Greek thought for the Romans. As a young man he had heard the heads of the three chief schools of Athens: Phaedrus the Epicurean, Diodotus the Stoic, and Philo the Academic. Under Philo's early influence he became an adherent of the New Academy, and remained one to the end of his life.

Of Cicero's philosophical works, none throws more light

upon his basic philosophy, and indirectly upon Arcesilaus and Carneades, than the *Academica,* in which he defends the Academic theory of knowledge against the followers of Antiochus. Cicero bases his scepticism upon Arcesilaus' demonstration "that no presentation proceeding from a true object is such that a presentation proceeding from a false one might not also be of the same form" (ii. 77) .[4] Following Carneades, he rejects the view that reason can act as a "distinguisher" between the false and the true, the real and the hallucinatory (ii. 91). At the same time he qualifies his scepticism with Academic probabilism, pointing out that "even many sense-percepts must be deemed probable, if only it be held in mind that no sense presentation has such a character as a false presentation could not also have without differing from it at all" (ii. 99). While, therefore, he shuns "that fierce wild beast, the act of assent," he is ready to follow probabilities "when nothing hampers." Assenting in this manner to what admittedly cannot be known is quite compatible, according to Cicero, with the highest wisdom (ii. 114).

While Cicero's efforts to revive the New Academy failed, Aenesidemus, a contemporary Greek philosopher, succeeded in reviving the long-defunct school of Pyrrho, although he was no doubt influenced by the New Academy also. The revival of Pyrrhonism lasted through the lifetime of Sextus Empiricus (about 160-210 A. D.), the author of the *Hypotyposes* and the *Adversus mathematicos.* The former work is a kind of summary of Greek scepticism, the latter an attack on dogmatism in various fields of knowledge. Though deriving his doctrines mainly from his predecessors, Sextus is representative of the "medical sceptics" of his own time. These were physicians as well as philosophers, and they held that the function of scepticism was therapeutic—to dispose of the dogmatists' ailment, self-conceit.

Of the many works produced by the Greek sceptics, only the two forementioned treatises by Sextus Empiricus have come down to the modern world. Our knowledge of ancient scepticism rests almost entirely on these two treatises, supplemented by the philosophical writings of Cicero and the *Lives of the Philosophers* by Diogenes Laertius. Though rediscovered in the Renaissance, these sources of information on ancient scepticism had no influence on the thought of the Middle Ages. In the thirteenth century, however, the Nominalists derived from the Arabian philosopher, Averroes, a doctrine reminiscent of the sceptical point of view in theology: this was the theory of the "two truths," that what is true in philosophy may be false in theology, and vice versa. Though repeatedly condemned by the ecclesiastical authorities,[5] the doctrine of the "two truths" persisted into the Renaissance.

Scepticism was revived in the Renaissance, along with other classical traditions. But Renaissance scepticism was not nearly so complex as the scepticism of anitiquity. From Cicero and Sextus Empiricus and Diogenes Laertius the Renaissance scholar merely gained a new insight into the limitations of human reason and applied this new insight to the religious problems of the time.

The most famous sceptic of the Renaissance, of course, was Montaigne. In his *Apologie for Raymond Sebond* Montaigne not only held that faith was the only safe foundation of religion, but also disparaged reason after the manner of the ancient sceptics by calling attention to the unreliability of our senses and the contradictory view of things taken by different philosophers. To illustrate the dangers of a religion based on reason Montaigne occasionally even went as far as Carneades, by presenting appeals to reason which supported atheism: "If God be, he is a living creature; if he is a living creature, he hath sense; and if he hath sense, he is subject to corruptions."[6] Though listed on the Prohibitory Index, Montaigne's *Essays* were conservative rather than anti-religious in purpose. But one of his disciples, Pierre Bayle, had considerable influence on the *philosophes* and contributed to the rise of French materialism.

The revival of scepticism on the continent did not have an immediate influence on English thought. Francis Bacon, for instance, adhered to the doctrine of the "two truths," which the revival of scepticism was rendering obsolete. Bacon placed three limitations upon human knowledge, of which one was "That we do not presume by the contemplation of nature to attain to the mysteries of God." Like the Western Averroists of the late Middle Ages, he emphasized the absolute separateness of "divinity" and "philosophy," cautioning men "that they do not unwisely mingle or confound these learnings together."[7] The virtue of this doctrine was that, on the one hand, it guarded against heresy and atheism, and on the other, it emancipated reason from ecclesiastical control.

Not until the publication of Sir Thomas Browne's *Religio Medici* in 1643 did the revival of ancient scepticism affect English thought. Though not unlike that of Montaigne, Browne's scepticism bears the mark of his own personality and is almost indistinguishable from his deep sense of the mystery of life: "Since I was of understanding to know we knew nothing, my reason hath been more pliable to the will of Faith; I am now content to understand a mystery without a rigid definition, in an easie Platonick description. The allegorical description of Hermes pleaseth me beyond all the Metaphysical definitions of Divines. Where I cannot satisfy my reason, I love to humour my fancy."[8] The ancient Academic tendency of claiming kinship with the greatest philosophers of the past culminates in Browne's feeling that "the wisest heads prove,

15

at last, almost all Scepticks, and stand like Janus in the field of knowledge" (p. 78).

During the Restoration some members of the Royal Society called attention to the limitations of reason in their polemics against the materialism of Hobbes.[9] Catholic propagandists had long employed the same argument against Protestantism, and soon Protestants like Joseph Butler and William Law were to use it against deism. But despite this diversity in its use, the scepticism of the enlightenment, until developed by David Hume, was hardly more elaborate than that of the Renaissance.

Though at length repudiated as a failure by its author, *A Treatise of Human Nature* is generally regarded as Hume's greatest work. An empiricism more thorough and consistent than Locke's forms the groundwork of this book. Hume referred to the primary data of knowledge as "impressions." Their "faint images," which we employ in thinking and reasoning, he called "ideas." The difference between the two is that "betwixt feeling and thinking."[10] Hume distinguished also between "original impressions" and "impressions of reflexion" or "internal impressions." By the former term he meant sensations arising from unknown causes; by the latter he meant passions, desires, and emotions arising either from original impressions or from ideas (I, 317, 460).

In rejecting innate ideas and basing knowledge on observation and experience, Hume followed the example of Locke. But while Locke avoided scepticism by assigning to reason the important function of operating on the materials of experience to produce knowledge, Hume subjected this function to a destructive analysis. In organizing the materials of experience into knowledge, the understanding, according to Hume, makes use of seven "philosophical relations"—resemblance, identity, space and time, proportions in quantity or number, degrees in quality, contrariety, and cause and effect (I, 322-

16

323). Of these seven relations, only one, that of cause and effect, "can lead us beyond the immediate impressions of our memory and senses" (I, 390). It follows, therefore, that causation is the foundation of rational knowledge. Accordingly, Hume subjected causation to a detailed and original analysis. The result of this analysis was to constitute his chief contribution to the history of thought. It was also to lay the basis of his scepticism.

Causation, according to Hume, is neither a self-evident principle nor a conclusion of *a priori* reasoning. We infer the existence of one object from that of another entirely from custom and experience. We remember, for example, to have seen that object called *flame* and to have felt that sensation called *heat*. At the same time we call to mind their constant conjunction in all past instances. Without further investigation, we call one cause and the other effect, and infer the existence of one from that of the other (I, 388). Beasts likewise draw such inferences from experience, though they never perceive any real connection between objects (I, 471). It follows, therefore, that the efficacy of causes belongs to the imagination, which gives the objects a necessary connection in the mind.

Hume dismissed as absurd the practice of defining the efficacy of causes by employing in the definition such synonyms of the term to be defined as agency, power, force, energy, necessity, connection, and productive quality (I, 451). The idea denoted by these synonymous terms must, according to Hume's principles, arise from some impression. It is not, however, derived from an impression conveyed by our senses. It must, therefore, arise from some internal impression. The only internal impression which suggests itself is "that propensity, which custom produces, to pass from an object to the idea of its usual attendant." This "propensity" is the essence of necessity, and it is "something that exists in the mind, not in objects." The efficacy or energy of causes, therefore, "belongs entirely to the soul, which considers the union of two or more objects in all past instances" (I, 460).

This analysis of causation inevitably led Hume to embrace scepticism. The ultimate aim of all our investigations, he pointed out, is to discover that energy in the cause by which it operates on its effect. What a great disappointment it must be, therefore, to learn that this energy lies in ourselves (I, 546). Thus reason tends to destroy itself: "When I reflect on the natural fallibility of my judgment, I have less confidence in my opinions, than when I consider the objects concerning which I reason; and when I proceed still further, to turn the scrutiny against every successive estimation I make of my faculties, all the rules of logic require a continual diminution, and at last a total extinction of belief and evidence" (I, 474).

Among the certitudes called in question by Hume's theory of causation were the ideas of the existence of an objective world, the existence of self, and the existence of a creative deity. Up to a certain point Hume's arguments against the belief in an external world are identical with Berkeley's. He agreed with Berkeley, for instance, in denying the distinction between so-called primary and secondary qualities—a distinction by which such qualities as extension and solidity were allowed to have an independent existence admittedly not shared by such qualities as color and sound, heat and cold (I, 510-516). Hume and Berkeley differ radically, however, in their answers to the argument that the existence of external objects had to be inferred, after all, as a cause of our perceptions. Though he held that unthinking matter could never be the cause of thought, Berkeley, no less than his adversaries, assumed a knowable cause, maintaining that "the cause of ideas is an incorporeal active substance or Spirit."[12] Hume, on the other hand, answered the argument of the dualists by holding that the causes of our original impressions are inexplicable and unknown. Nothing, Hume pointed out, is ever present to the mind but perceptions; we may, therefore, "observe a conjunction or a relation of cause and effect between different perceptions, but can never observe it between perceptions and objects" (I, 499-500). Regarded as the cause of our perceptions, spirit, according to Hume's principles, is quite as meaningless as matter.

A consequence of this difference between Hume and Berkeley appears in their discussion of the question of real objects and creations of the fancy. Our perception of "real things," according to Berkeley, has its cause in God and is independent of our will; our perception of "chimeras," on the other hand, has no such superior cause but is dependent only upon ourselves (I, 173). But Hume, limiting causation to a relation among perceptions, was unable to find any such essential distinction between these two classes of objects. The ideas of the memory, according to Hume, are simply "more strong and lively" than the ideas of the imagination (I, 385). "An idea assented to *feels* different from a fictitious idea" (I, 398).

Applying his theory of causation to the idea of self, as he had applied it to the idea of an external world, Hume arrived at another sceptical conclusion. The idea of self, he pointed out, cannot be derived from an impression, since that impression would have to continue invariably the same from our birth to our death, and no such impression exists (I, 533). What we call the self, then, turns out to be "nothing but a bundle or collection of different perceptions, which succeed each other in an inconceivable rapidity and are in a perpetual flux and movement" (I, 534). The idea of self cannot be a bond among these various perceptions since the understanding can never observe any real connection among any objects whatever. Identity, therefore, is not a uniting principle belonging to our perceptions; it is merely an accomplishment of the fancy, in which ideas are united because of their constant conjunction (I, 540).

Hume's theory of causation led to scepticism also regarding the idea of a creative deity. From the resemblance of the universe to a machine, Cleanthes, one of the disputants in the *Dialogues Concerning Natural Religion*, infers "at once the existence of a Deity, and his similarity to human mind and intelligence" (II, 392). But this argument, according to Hume's theory of knowledge, was defective even aside from the question of the efficacy of causes, for it assumed a constant conjunction of objects of which we have absolutely no experience. "To ascertain this reasoning," replies Philo, the sceptic, "it is requisite that we had experience of the origin of worlds; and it is not sufficient surely, that we have seen ships and cities arise from human contrivance" (II, 398).

But of what value is this destructive reasoning, this scepticism that deprives us of the idea of an objective world, the idea of self, and the idea of a Supreme Intelligence? Hume distinguished at least two benefits to be derived from scepticism. First, it serves as an antidote to dogmatism, narrow-mindedness, and conceit. Secondly, it helps to "undermine the foundations of an abstruse philosophy, which seems to have hitherto served only a shelter to superstition, and a cover to absurdity and error!" To appreciate the significance Hume attached to this second benefit, one must consider his theory of the bad influence of superstition on morals. The superstitious man, according to Hume, does not recognize that the best way to serve God is by serving mankind; he is liable, therefore, not only to fall into some useless way of expressing his devotion—such as fasting a day or giving himself a whipping, but also to view such piety as compatible with the greatest crimes.[13]

While Hume defended the negative result of scepticism on the ground that it undermined dogmatism and superstition, he was aware, like the sceptics of the past, that even a sceptic must hold opinions and act on them. Adherence to a total scepticism, according to the *Treatise,* was impossible because nature had determined us "to judge as well as to breathe and feel" (I, 474-475). Our positive judgments, however, do not rest on reason alone. The sceptic is rescued from total scepticism by means of the imagination. Without the aid of the imagination, reason "can never give rise to any original idea" (I, 452). The imagination, too, is "the ultimate judge of all systems of philosophy." Why, then, blame the ancient philosophers for "allowing themselves to be entirely guided by it in their reasonings?" Hume distinguished between the permanent and universal principles of the imagination such as the customary transition from causes to effects and the "weak" and "changeable" principles such as substance, accident, and occult qualities (I, 510-511). The latter principles of the imagination, producing that "abstruse philosophy" which sheltered superstition, Hume regarded as objectionable; but the former principles were necessary to avoid all extinction of belief.

As the imagination is necessary, according to Hume, in the creation of knowledge, so the passions are necessary in the motivation of the will. The will is that internal impression which we feel "when we knowingly give rise to any new motion of our body, or new perception of our mind" (II, 181). Now all that we know about necessity in the actions of matter— the constant conjunction of objects and the inference from the existence of one to that of the other—is found also in all the operations of the mind (II, 185). It follows, therefore, that the will cannot be free, as all its actions have particular causes. Except for such a doctrine of necessity, no one could be blamed or praised for his conduct, as his acts would "proceed from nothing in him that is durable or constant." Liberty in this case would be synonymous with chance (II, 191-192).

Hume found the particular causes of the actions of the will not in the judgments of the understanding but in the passions. On this point Spinoza, Francis Hutcheson, and Joseph Butler had anticipated him,[14] but he fitted the doctrine to his own thought and purpose. The passions stood for that certitude of nature which overcomes the sceptic's doubts and renders action not only possible but unavoidable. Taking, therefore, a stand opposed to "the greatest part of moral philosophy, ancient and modern," he sought "to prove *first*, that reason alone can never be a motive to any action of the will; and *secondly*, that it can never oppose passion in the direction of the will" (II, 193). In human conduct reason can function only as "the slave of the passions" (II, 195). This fact may escape us because while "violent passions" are easily recognized, "calm passions" are often mistaken for determinations of reason. Besides, passions do not influence the will in proportion to their violence: a passion that has become "a settled principle of action" may, in fact, produce "no sensible agitation at all" (II, 197-198).

Upon this theory of the passions Hume erected both his ethics and his religion. Since moral principles obviously excite passions and cause or prevent actions, they cannot be the conclusions of reason, for "reason is perfectly inert, and can never either prevent or produce any action or affection" (II, 235). It follows, therefore, that moral principles have their source in our feelings. Hume traced the origin of our ideas of vice and virtue to the pleasure or pain arising from

22

our contemplation of particular actions: "Every quality of the mind is denominated virtuous which gives pleasure by the mere survey; as every quality which produces pain is called vicious" (II, 348). The pleasure or pain which we feel in the contemplation of actions, however, is regulated by that "powerful principle of human nature" called sympathy. Sympathy, then, is the chief source of moral distinctions (II, 371).

Hume's theology, in the final analysis, rests likewise on his theory of the passions, so that his contradictory remarks on religion are not fundamentally irreconcilable. No theological demonstration, as we noted above, was allowed to stand by Hume on the negative side of his scepticism, which was based wholly on reason. But as the Academic sceptics were ready to assent to the "probable," so Hume was willing to yield "to that propensity, which inclines us to be positive and certain in *particular points,* according to the light, in which we survey them in any *particular instant*" (I, 552). When he felt like it, therefore, he could assert that "the whole frame of nature bespeaks an intelligent author," though he himself had clearly pointed out the defect of this argument. Occasionally, on the other hand, Hume echoed the Renaissance sceptics: "Our most holy religion is founded on *Faith,* not reason. . . ."[15] But whether he yielded to a "propensity" to accept a theological argument or argued that religion rests not on reason but "Faith," Hume was in each case, after all, basing religion ultimately on the feelings.

III

SHELLEY'S SIR WILLIAM DRUMMOND

SHELLEY does not comment on all the sceptics mentioned in the preceding chapter. But he comments on some of them, and, with but one exception, in each case the comment constitutes a remarkable tribute. Hume's *Essays,* according to Thomas Jefferson Hogg,[1] "were a favorite book with Shelley" at Oxford; and even in *A Defence of Poetry* (1819), where Shelley's purpose was to glorify poets and not metaphysicians, Hume is placed among those who "are entitled to the gratitude of mankind" (VII, 133). In a letter to Hogg, dated November 13, 1813, Shelley refers to Cicero as "one of the most admirable characters the world ever produced." Charging French literature with superficiality, Shelley qualifies the charge by citing two notable exceptions—of whom one was Montaigne (VII, 13-14). The only sceptic whom Shelley disliked, so far as I know, was Pierre Bayle, the precursor of the French materialists, because of his "obliquity of understanding and coarseness of feeling" (IX, 119). But perhaps Shelley's tributes to the great sceptics of the past are not so significant as his admiration for a now little known sceptic of his own day.

Sir William Drummond possessed a wide variety of notable talents: among other things he was a diplomat, a classical scholar, a student of the Old Testament, and a philosopher. He is remembered today, however, primarily as a metaphysician admired by Shelley. Condemning the philosophy of his time as superstitious or sophistical, the poet added in a footnote to the preface to *The Revolt of Islam*: "I ought to except Sir W. Drummond's 'Academical Questions;' a volume of very acute and powerful metaphysical criticism." In a letter to Leigh Hunt dated November 3, 1819, Shelley paid tribute to Drummond in almost the same words, describing him as "the most acute metaphysical critic of the age." But even more significant than this high estimate of Drummond is Shelley's observation in the essay *On Life* [1819][2] that the *Academical Questions* was perhaps the most lucid exposition of the "intellectual system"—a system which, the poet implied, included his own philosophical position (VI, 194-195).

In view of these well known facts an accurate interpretation of Drummond's *Academical Questions* must be regarded as of some importance in any effort to understand the metaphysical views of Shelley. This statement, of course, would not hold true in the event that Shelley had misinterpreted the *Academical Questions*. But the danger of such a result was less in his case than it is in ours, for he dealt with a distinguished contemporary, while we deal with a philosopher of the past whom historians of philosophy have ignored.

Elaborating Mary Shelley's remark that "Shelley was a disciple of the Immaterial Philosophy of Berkeley,"[3] G. S. Brett in 1931 pointed out that the philosophy of Berkeley came to Shelley "through the medium of Drummond's book,"[4] a view that has gained wide acceptance.[5] It is not my purpose to question Berkeley's influence on Drummond, but to suggest that the basic influence on Drummond came from a different source. I shall here attempt to demonstrate two things: first, that Drummond was fundamentally a disciple not of Berkeley but of Hume; secondly, that Shelley, like his contemporaries, recognized Drummond as a sceptic—that is, as a philososopher who stressed the limitations of the human mind and the uncertainty of all knowledge. The present subject, then, is the *Academical Questions* and Shelley's understanding of a work that he admired. What influence Drummond and the sceptical tradition had on the poet's philosophy will be the subject of later chapters.

Historians of philosophy are no doubt justified in overlooking Drummond; his philosophical doctrines not only were derivative but had no influence on the main stream of British thought. Nevertheless, he possessed a kind of originality— the originality that belongs to opposing the main tendencies of one's time. To understand Drummond's purpose one ought first to consider the development of dogmatism in British philosophy during the forty years preceding the publication of the *Academical Questions* (London, 1805).

Although Hume's sceptical conclusions were profoundly to affect European thought, they won him critics rather than disciples. Hume's greatest critic, of course, was Kant; but neither Kant nor the later German transcendentalists had any appreciable influence on English philosophers—unless Coleridge be included under that classification—before the middle of the nineteenth century.[6] Before that time the main critics of Hume in England belonged to the Common Sense school.

In his *Enquiry into the Human Mind* (1765), Thomas Reid, the founder of the Common Sense school, endeavored to refute Hume by attacking Hume's premises. Hume's sceptical conclusions, according to Reid, are inevitable inferences from the "ideal" theory—a theory traceable ultimately to Descartes—"that every object of thought must be an impression or an idea." On the basis of this theory, according to Reid, Locke was able to deny the existence of the secondary qualities of bodies, Berkeley to deny the existence of matter altogether, and Hume to deny the existence of both matter and spirit. Reid attacked, therefore, not only Hume but all "the doctors of this ideal philosophy." He found but one alternative to the acceptance of Hume's sceptical conclusions: to recognize that the inferences which we draw from our sensations are "judgments of nature—judgments not got by comparing ideas, and perceiving agreements and disagreements, but immediately inspired by our constitution."[7]

Among Reid's immediate disciples were George Campbell, James Oswald, and James Beattie. While none of these men possessed any originality as philosophers, one of them—James Beattie—won great popular acclaim. Beattie's *Essay on Truth* (1770) added to Reid's argument against Hume the spirit of infuriated piety. The impression it made upon the reading public of the 1770s is exemplified by Joshua Reynolds' famous painting wherein Beattie clasps his *Essay on Truth* with Olympian serenity while the sinister figures representing Hume and his intellectual companions are hurled into limbo.[8]

The success of the Common Sense school in discrediting scepticism is apparent in the next thirty-five years, not only in the works of Dugald Stewart, the most distinguished exponent of the Common Sense school among Drummond's contemporaries, but also in the works of the Utilitarians. Despite his indebtedness to Hume's theory of morals, Jeremy Bentham ignored Hume's metaphysics and, in effect, sided with the dogmatists. In the midst of this triumph of dogmatism Drummond, like Cicero in the first century B. C., made an unsuccessful effort to revive scepticism.

The very title of Drummond's philosophical treatise suggests the sceptical philosophy. Originally the name of a grove where Plato taught, the term "Academy" was first applied to Plato's school. His successors—Arcesilaus, Carneades, Philo of Larissa—who were not Platonists but sceptics, constituted the "New Academy." Cicero called his defence of this sceptical philosophy the *Academica,* while later St. Augustine called his attack on it *Contra Academicos.* It is in this last sense that the term "Academical" has been used by modern philosophers: the twelfth section of Hume's *An Enquiry Concerning the Human Understanding,* for instance, is entitled "Of the Academical or Sceptical Philosophy." It is incredible that Drummond, who was a classical scholar as well as a philosopher, was unfamiliar with this meaning of "Academical" in ancient and modern philosophy. It is also incredible that he was unaware of the analogies between his *Academical Questions* and Cicero's *Academica.*

Drummond's *Academical Questions,* like Cicero's *Academica,* marked an effort to revive the scepticism of a preceding age in opposition to the dogmatic temper of one's contemporaries. The foundation of the dogmatism of Drummond's contemporaries, as we noted above, was the success of the Common Sense school in discrediting the epistemological achievements of modern philosophy from Descartes through Hume. Interpreting this movement begun by Reid as fundamentally an attack on philosophy itself, Drummond was able to say in the Preface: "Of the prejudices, which now exist in this country against philosophical speculations, every writer, who indulges himself in them, ought to be aware" (pp. ii-iv). That he had in mind the "prejudices" created by the Common Sense school, and tacitly shared by the Utilitarians, is apparent when he goes on to say that "the study of the human mind, which is the study of human nature, and that examination of the principles which is so necessary to the scrutiny of truth, are either discouraged as dangerous, or neglected as useless" (p. viii).

To undermine the foundation of the dogmatism of his age, Drummond chose to refute the dogmatic belief in the existence of matter. It is this aspect of his work, more than any other element in it, that has led to the misleading association of Drummond with Berkeley. What Shelley's critics have entirely overlooked is that Hume also had refuted this dogma, employing an original argument. To Berkeley's objection to the distinction between primary qualities and secondary (the former allegedly having an existence independent of perception), Hume added, as we noted in the preceding chapter, an argument not found in Berkeley—an argument suggested to him by his analysis of cause. Now which of these two arguments did Drummond deem the more important?

Drummond admitted that his conclusion regarding matter was similar to Berkeley's conclusion. He pointed out, however, that he had arrived at his conclusion "by a different induction" from that of the Bishop of Cloyne (p. 70). This "different induction" is illustrated in the following passage:

> It may be asked how I account for sensations, if I question the existence of a material *substratum?* . . . To assign causes for everything has been the vain attempt of ignorance in every age. It has been by encouraging this error, that superstition has enslaved the world. In proportion as men are rude, uncultivated, and uncivilized, they are determined in their opinions, bold in their presumptions and obstinate in their prejudices. When they begin to doubt, it may be concluded,

they begin to be refined.   The savage is seldom a sceptic
—the barbarian is rarely incredulous. (p. 39)

In other words, the argument against materialism which Drummond found most convincing was Hume's argument: we cannot assume matter to account for the source of our sensations
because these arise from unknown causes.

The significance of this "different induction" lies in its
consequence, which sharply distinguishes Drummond from
Berkeley. Berkeley refuted the materialistic hypothesis, it
will be recalled, in order to maintain that "the cause of our
ideas is an incorporeal active substance or Spirit." By assuming a knowable cause in this fashion, Berkeley was able to
distinguish clearly between "real things" and "chimeras," the
former class of objects having their cause in God and being
independent of our wills, the latter having no such superior
cause but being dependent upon the beholder. Hume, on the
other hand, recognized no essential distinction between these
two classes of objects because he rejected Berkeley's assumption of cause. Drummond followed Hume: "A lunatic may
be persuaded that all mankind agree with him, in the wildest
fables. . . . Nevertheless the conviction of the philosopher,
like that of the lunatic, has no support but from itself" (p.
152). Only such a conclusion was consistent with the grounds
upon which Drummond rejected materialism.

It is apparent, therefore, that Drummond refuted materialism as a sceptic, not as a Berkeleian idealist; for if no
absolute distinction exists between "real things" and hallucina-
tions, then how can we ever be certain of the soundness of
our opinions on any subject whatsoever? In this manner
Drummond's refutation of materialism leads to the central
theme of the *Academical Questions*—an argument directed
against the dogmatic temper of the age:

Now what is to prove to the individual the infallible certainty of any proposition? When I consider my own mind, and when I recollect, that my own consciousness is the ultimate test, to which I can appeal, I fear to pronounce, that in me exists a standard of immutable truth. Since I have begun to reason, I have often felt and lamented the insufficiency of my judgment. My experience, as far as it can instruct me, shows me the very limited powers of human understanding; and instead of rendering me confident in my belief, makes me deeply sensible of the uncertainty of all my knowledge. (p. 154)

Drummond's indebtedness to Hume and to the traditions of scepticism is apparent also in other doctrines of the *Academical Questions*. Drummond's discussion of Necessity is a paraphrase of Hume's treatment of that subject discussed in the preceding chapter. Like Hume, Drummond denied that we have any knowledge of the efficacy of causes: "To suppose the existence of power at all may, perhaps, be nothing else than the hypothesis of men, who admit the occult operation of something, which is no object of understanding, for the purpose of accounting for events" (p. 180). If, therefore, we assume Necessity in the case of "physical causes," we ought to be consistent, allowing it also in the case of "moral motives," for all we know in either case is the "constant association of certain events" (pp. 191-192).

Denying free will upon sceptical grounds, Hume was led to place the motives actuating the will, as we have previously noted, not in the judgments of the understanding but in the emotions, regarding reason in human conduct as "the slave of the passions." Though this theory of the passions was a commonplace in eighteenth-century thought, by relating it to his sceptical philosophy Hume gave it a new significance. Drummond, therefore, probably owed something to Hume's treatment of the theory when he observed that "reason, or will, or any other faculty, which may be supposed to influence the mind, can only control passion, as one sentiment controls another" (p. 17).

Finally, Drummond's treatment of theological questions agrees with the sceptical tradition in general and with Cicero's *De natura deorum* and Hume's *Dialogues Concerning Natural Religion* in particular. In his *Oedipus Judaicus,* an effort by Drummond to interpret the Old Testament allegorically, occurs the following fideistic passage, not without parallels in Cicero and Hume, but perhaps more reminiscent of the Renaissance sceptics: "I must yet confess, that I like better the humility of those, who bow with blind reverence to the sacred Oracles, in acknowledging the difficulty of comprehending them; than the arrogance of certain teachers, who, adhering to the literal sense of the scriptures, boldly pronounce, that every event recorded in them is probable, and consisent with the plans of eternal wisdom."[9]

But in Chapter IV of the *Academical Questions* Drummond employs the ironical method of Cicero and Hume: the arguments form part of a dialogue and the author's point remains ambiguous and elusive—except the point that there is no rational certitude in religion. This is the point of Chapter IV of the *Academical Questions*—a point which supports the theme of the book as a whole. The dialogue consists mainly in a debate between Theophilus, one of those pious dogmatists "who fear nothing so much as that they should seem to doubt anything" (p. 218), and Hylas, who with equal dogmatism recognizes "no agency but Nature's, and no deity but matter" (p. 278). Eugenius, who may be said to speak for Drummond, avers his belief in God and the soul's immortality, but rejects the dogmatic arguments of Theophilus (p. 281).

Thus the title, the Preface, and the basic doctrines of the *Academical Questions* suggest but one conclusion: that Drummond was a sceptic and a disciple of Hume. It remains now to be shown that Drummond's contemporaries recognized him as a sceptic. The reviewer[10] of the *Academical Questions* for the *Edinburgh Review* in 1805 said of its author: "The subjects of his investigation are so various, his criticism so unsparing, and his conclusions so hostile to every species of dogmatism, that we have sometimes been tempted to think, that he had no other view in this publication, than to expose the weakness of human understanding" (VII, 164). The reviewer also found Drummond to be especially dissatisfied with the Common Sense philosophy (p. 170) and classified his thought as "speculative scepticism" (p. 175).

A similar interpretation of the *Academical Questions* appeared in *The British Critic* in 1806. Drummond was described as "calling in question every received truth, and undermining the foundation of every system of science" (XXVII, 13). Though aware of Berkeley's influence on Hume (p. 14), the reviewer regarded Drummond as Hume's disciple rather than Berkeley's: "Berkeley did not, like Hume and the present author, call in question the existence of the human soul, or deny that we have any notion of *power*" (p. 14, note).

In Shelley's first reference to the *Academical Questions*, which occurs in the Notes to *Queen Mab* (I, 150-151), he specifically recognized Drummond as a sceptic but charged him with being inconsistent: "Had this author, instead of inveighing against the guilt and absurdity of atheism, demonstrated its falsehood, his conduct would have been more suited to the modesty of the sceptic and the toleration of a philosopher." There would be no point in saying that a difference in the conduct of a man would have been more suited to "the modesty of the sceptic" unless one recognized in him some claim to that title. That the word "sceptic," furthermore, was here used by Shelley in the sense in which we are using it is apparent both from its juxtaposition to "modesty," a virtue traditionally claimed by sceptics, and from the fact that the popular sense of the term "sceptic"—one who disbelieves in Christianity—would render Shelley's remark absurdly contradictory.

While none of Shelley's later references to Drummond contains the word "sceptic," they contain evidence that the poet continued to think of Drummond as fundamentally a sceptic. More important than the evidence just considered, for instance, is the following passage in *A Refutation of Deism*:

> Hume has shewn, to the satisfaction of all philosophers, that the only idea which we can form of causation is derivable from the constant conjunction of objects, and the consequent inference from the one to the other. We denominate that phenomenon the cause of another which we observe with the fewest exceptions to precede its occurrence. Hence it would be inadmissible to deduce the being of God from the existence of the Universe, even if this mode of reasoning did not conduct to the monstrous conclusion of an infinity of creative and created Gods, each more eminently requiring a Creator than its predecessor.
> If Power be an attribute of existing substance, substance could not have derived its origin from power. One thing cannot be at the same time the cause and the effect of another. (VI, 55)

As Shelley's reference to Hume indicates, the basic concept in this passage is Hume's theory of cause or power—a concept that is here applied in various ways to a theological question. The sly and ambiguous phrase "to the satisfaction of all philosophers" cannot be taken literally, but there can be no doubt that Hume's theory at least met with the approval of Drummond. In a footnote to the term "Power" in the second paragraph Shelley added: "For a very profound disquisition on this subject, see Sir William Drummond's *Academical Questions*, chap. i. p. 1." The passage and the footnote, when read together, clearly establish the poet's awareness of Drummond's indebtedness to Hume.

In his essay *On Life* Shelley classified Drummond as an expounder of the "Intellectual Philosophy," a phrase which critics have often referred to but have not satisfactorily explained. The phrase, to be sure, suggests some form of Platonic or Neo-Platonic idealism—and therefore the philosophy of Berkeley. But it is doubtful that Shelley primarily intended to convey that suggestion. Hume's *Treatise* had employed the terms "intellectual world" and "ideal world" (I, 516, 541) to distinguish the realm of ideas from the realm of what Kant was to call things-in-themselves. Reid, as we noted earlier, attacked the "ideal system," by which he meant a principle in the philosophy of Descartes, Locke, Berkeley, and Hume. Drummond refers to his own philosophy not only as sceptical but also as "ideal" and "intellectual," using these terms as Hume and Hume's opponents had used them.[11] By the "Intellectual Philosophy," therefore, Shelley must have meant the philosophy attacked by the Common Sense school—the philosophy that reached its fullest development in the scepticism of Hume.

This interpretation of Shelley's phrase is confirmed by his own explanation: "It is difficult to find terms adequate to express so subtle a conception as that to which the Intellectual Philosophy has conducted us. We are on the verge where words abandon us, and what wonder if we grow dizzy to look down the dark abyss of how little we know" (VI, 196). To his own question as to what follows the admission of the main conclusions of the "Intellectual Philosophy," the poet replied: "It establishes no new truth, it gives us no additional insight into our hidden nature, neither its action or itself. Philosophy, impatient as it may be to build, has much work yet remaining, as pioneer for the overgrowth of ages. It makes one step toward this object; it destroys error, and the roots of error. It leaves, what is too often the duty of the reformer in political and ethical questions to leave, a vacancy" (VI, 195). In *On the Punishment of Death* the poet substituted another name for the "Intellectual Philosophy," calling it the "modern Academy," a school of thought which reveals to us "the prodigious depth and extent of our ignorance respecting the causes and nature of sensation" (VI, 185).

Shelley, then, appears to have recognized Drummond for what he was—a sceptic. One pertinent question, however, remains to be dealt with. Why did the poet in the Notes to *Queen Mab* charge Drummond with being an inconsistent sceptic and later refrain from repeating this charge?

The poet's early charge against Drummond probably resulted from his misinterpretation of Chapter IV of the *Academical Questions,* a chapter consisting in a dialogue on theological questions. Shelley apparently assumed that one of the two main disputants was voicing the author's opinions. Recognizing that these could not be identified with those of Hylas, the materialist, the poet identified the author's views with those of Theophilus, the theosophist. The real purpose of the dialogue—to expose dogmatism in theology, be the speaker religious or anti-religious—at first escaped the young poet, who therefore drew the logical conclusion that Drummon's scepticism was inconsistent. Perhaps it was Shelley's misinterpretation of this part of the *Academical Questions* that led him to suspect the purpose of *Oedipus Judaicus* (to Thomas Hookham, January 24, 1813), Drummond's quite unorthodox interpretation of the Old Testament.

If Shelley, as appears to have been the case, was soon to revise his interpretation of Chapter IV of the *Academical*

Questions, he probably did so as a result of his enhanced knowledge of the traditions of scepticism. Prior to the publication of *Queen Mab* (1813) Shelley's knowledge of scepticism was confined to some of Hume's Essays and Drummond's *Academical Questions.* But by 1817 he not only had reread Hume and probably Drummond as well, but had become acquainted with the main types of scepticism in the history of European thought: with Pyrrhonism through reading the chapter on Pyrrho in Diogenes Laertius, with the New Academy through reading the philosophical writings of Cicero, with Renaissance scepticism through reading Sir Thomas Browne's *Religio Medici* and Montaigne's *An Apology of Raymond Sebond.*[12] The turning point in Shelley's attitude toward Drummond probably occurred in the fall of 1813, when he read many of Cicero's philosophical works, no doubt including the *De natura deorum,* referred to in *A Refutation of Deism* (VI, 30). Cicero's *De natura,* the only treatise surviving from antiquity which illustrates Carneades' ironical method of treating theological problems, was the prototype of both Hume's *Dialogues Concerning Natural Religion* and Drummond's theological dialogue in the *Academical Questions.* Shelley himself immediately adopted this ironical method in *A Refutation of Deism* (1814), and it is significant that his first tribute to Drummond occurs in a footnote of this work (VI, 55).

Since Drummond appears to have been a sceptic, and since Shelley and other contemporaries appear to have regarded him as such, the widely held view that the poet became a follower of Berkeley by reading Drummond seems to require considerable modification. That Shelley was a disciple of Berkeley is still, of course, supported by the authority of Mary Shelley. It is quite possible, however, that her remark had a somewhat different meaning for her than it has for us. The positive side of Berkeley's thought, that is, his idealism, was little heeded in England during Mary Shelley's lifetime. Reid and his followers had created the tradition of considering Berkeley, despite his expressed opposition to scepticism in his Introduction to the *Principles of Human Knowledge,* as merely a precursor of Hume. Mary Shelley's appreciation of Berkeley does not appear to have been in advance of that of her age. Thus after stating that Shelley was a disciple of Berkeley, she elaborated her remark by discussing a poem in which Shelley "expresses his despair of being able to conceive, far less express, all the variety, majesty, and beauty, which is veiled from our imperfect senses in the unknown realm, the mystery of which his poetic vision sought in vain to penetrate." To my mind, Mary Shelley's remark suggests the influence of Hume quite as much as the influence of Berkeley.

It cannot be denied that Berkeley influenced Drummond; in fact, it cannot be denied that Berkeley influenced Hume. But there is to be found in Drummond a tendency toward idealism essentially foreign to Hume—a tendency that has some affinity with the "ideas" of Plato and the idealism of Berkeley. This tendency goes beyond the result of denying the existence of the material world; in other words, it is positive rather than negative in character. Critics in the past, however, have exaggerated this element in Drummond. They have also, possibly, misinterpreted it, for its peculiar character may very well depend on its relation to Drummond's scepticism.

The sceptical tradition, it should be remembered, has its positive as well as its negative side. The ancient Pyrrhonists reconciled doubt and the inevitability of entertaining opinions by relying on custom, the New Academy by expounding a doctrine of probability—the doctrine that, while no knowledge is certain, propositions differ in the degree to which they have the "appearance" of truth. Most Renaissance sceptics recommended faith as a solution to doubt. Hume, in a manner of speaking, returned to the probabilism of the New Academy. His probabilism, however, took two forms, profoundly different in effect if not in principle.

Far from being an obstacle to the development of science, Hume's scepticism actually contributed to a wider application of the scientific method by concentrating rational enquiry upon the "constant conjunction of objects" discoverable only through observation and experiment. Hume did not hesitate to give qualified assent to logical conclusions regarding this world of appearance, nor did science require more than what he granted. This was one of the forms taken by Hume's probabilism. The other form had to do, not with the world of appearance, but with ultimate reality. Since this realm of being lay beyond any possible observation of the "constant conjunction of objects," we cannot properly reason about it. But Hume sometimes exhibits a willingness to give qualified assent also to conclusions regarding the unknowable, basing his right to do so on the imagination or feeling. Thus in the conclusion of the *Dialogues Concerning Natural Religion* Philo, who speaks for Hume, ironically embraces the deism which he had just refuted. Thus, too, Hume sometimes recommends faith as the foundation of religion.

To Drummond, as to Hume, ultimate reality was unknowable. It is quite possible, therefore, that Drummond's idealism rested, like the deistic and fideistic elements in Hume, on a form of probabilism which gave imagination and feeling their due. This conclusion seems the more likely when we consider the hostility of the *Academical Questions* (351 ff.) to the transcendentalists—an hostility otherwise difficult to explain. According to Drummond's fundamentally sceptical principles, a dogmatic idealism would be inadmissible: that is why he rejects the transcendentalists along with the materialists. That Drummond based his idealism upon the second form of probabilism noted in Hume is further supported by Drummond's ambivalent attitude toward Plato. He finds fault with Plato as well as with Aristotle for indulging "too much in conjecture" and asserting "what experience does not confirm" (p. 2); at the same time he grants that the word "idea" may have a "higher meaning" than the sense in which he generally understands it, and does not "deny the existence of divine and intelligible ideas, as those were explained by Plato, to be possible" (p. xiv). This ambivalent attitude toward Plato is in the sceptical tradition. What Drummond therefore perhaps meant, as his term "possible" likewise suggests, was that certain Platonic conceptions, though not verifiable by reason, might still have for the sceptic the "appearance" or "feeling" of truth. In other words, Drummond suggests that he would have based the positive side of his thought on probability or faith. There are traces of these principles, as we have noted, in Hume also. It never occurrd to Hume, however, to apply them to the "ideas" of Plato.

The positive side of Drummond's thought exhibits other deviations from Hume toward a greater degree of idealism. Though he denies, for instance, the existence of liberty understood as "*a power of self-motion, or self-determination,*" Drummond is more concerned than Hume appears to be in distinguishing his doctrine from that of the typical eighteenth-century necessarian, who was generally a materialist: "The advocates of necessity contend, that the will must necessarily be determined in its choice by the strongest motive. Now, it is evident, that they found this argument upon the supposed necessary connexion between cause and effect; and if this be not admitted, there is an end of their doctrine" (p. 192).

Unsympathetic toward the work they were reviewing, Drummond's contemporary critics, as we have already noted, tended to ignore the peculiar character of the *Academical Questions*—its effort to reconcile empiricism and idealism: they regarded it as largely a restatement of the ideas of Hume. Shelley's critics, on the other hand, have ignored Drummond's scepticism and overemphasized his idealism. For a true understanding of Drummond we must combine these two antagonistic interpretations. Like Berkeley, Drummond seeks to reconcile empiricism and idealism; his method of doing so, however, is derived not from Berkeley but from the sceptical tradition. Drummond is fundamentally a sceptic who tends toward a provisional idealism.

Since Shelley clearly regarded himself as a follower of the tradition represented in his own day by Drummond, was he also a sceptic who pursued a non-dogmatic idealism compatible with scepticism? An attempt to answer this question will be made in the ensuing chapters. It ought to be mentioned at this point, however, that Drummond never fully elaborated the positive side of his thought: he intended to perform this task in a second volume of the *Academical Questions,* which, if ever written, was never published. In attempting, therefore, to reconcile empiricism and idealism Shelley probably desired more help from Drummond than Drummond gave.

IV

SCEPTICISM AND IMMATERIALISM

ONE of the most important developments in Shelley's intellectual history was his rejection of what has been called his juvenile materialism. Newman I. White observes that this development occurred at about the same time as the disastrous consequences of the poet's first marriage,[1] that is, during the years 1814-1816. This suggestion is acceptable regarding the final and most conspicuous phase of the whole process, but other phases of it are traceable to an earlier period. At all events the Platonism that strongly colors Shelley's thought after 1817 must be interpreted as an effect rather than a cause of the poet's rejection of materialism. Accordingly, many critics have correctly sought the major influence behind Shelley's rejection of materialism in English philosophers of the eighteenth and the early nineteenth centuries. By interpreting Drummond as a disciple of Berkeley, they have established Berkeley as the main influence behind Shelley's rejection of materialism. The widespread acceptance of this theory, however, has led, and will continue to lead, to the discovery of alleged inconsistencies in the poet's thought.

These charges of inconsistency take various forms. One type is illustrated by the remark of Benjamin P. Kurtz that "if Shelley ever really thought he was a disciple of Berkeley, he was a confused disciple, as I have tried to show."[2] A more common charge of inconsistency, however, arises from the persistence in Shelley of influences associated with his juvenile materialism, existing side by side with his alleged Berkeleian immaterialism. I. J. Kapstein, for instance, finds such an irreconcilable conflict disrupting the unity of *Mont Blanc* (1816) : "Up to the last three lines of the poem Shelley's attitude is awe and worship of the remote, amoral power of Necessity ruling eternally the mutable universe of matter and the human mind. Of this power the towering peak of Mont Blanc is the central symbol of the poem. Shelley's submission to the rule of Necessity is sustained up to the last three lines of the poem, but in the course of his exposition of the doctrine he balks in a number of crucial places at accepting it. The reluctance implicit in the confused and ambiguous phrasing finally becomes explicit in the last three lines; here with a shift of attitude from worship to defiance of the power of Necessity, Shelley's logic also shifts, so that in contradiction of what he has been saying for a hundred and forty-one lines he brings the poem to an anti-climax." Though Mr. Kapstein feels that Shelley later became a more consistent exponent of Berkeleian immaterialism, he admits the "curious persistence" of the poet's necessarianism.[3]

It is my hypothesis that the confusion of ideas found in Shelley by many of his critics results from their failure to consider his relation to the sceptical tradition. The charges just mentioned, for instance, all depend upon the assumption that

Shelley was a disciple of Berkeley—a disciple who either distorted his master's immaterialism or mingled it incongruously with Holbach, Godwin, and the doctrine of Necessity. The present chapter will challenge this assumption by attempting to demonstrate the following: first, that Shelley rejected materialism upon sceptical grounds traceable to Hume; secondly, that this scepticism did not conflict with the poet's political radicalism and Godwin's influence; and thirdly, that Shelley's immaterialism and necessarianism are quite compatible as aspects of a basically sceptical philosophy.

Hume's influence on Shelley's anti-religious sentiments is well known. But because the poet's anti-religious sentiments are often associated with his early materialism, it has appeared to some critics that Hume, instead of emancipating the young poet from a rigid and dogmatic way of thinking, contributed to the genesis of that mode of thinking. Thus Amiyakumar Sen, who investigated Hume's influence on Shelley in some detail, concluded that the Scotch philosopher conducted the young poet from the philosophy of Locke to the "materialism of the French School."[4] But as Shelley's anti-religious views are by no means peculiar to the materialist period of his thought, the logical conclusion would seem to be that any connection between those anti-religious sentiments and the materialism of the poet's youth is essentially fortuitous—and therefore misleading. What, then, do we mean by Shelley's early materialism?

Shelley's early materialism may be divided into three doctrines: first, that spirit can be explained in terms of matter and motion; secondly, that reason is the sole guide to truth; and thirdly, that external objects possess a reality independent of perception. These three doctrines, it should be noted, are not inseparable from one another; in fact, they are not even necessarily related. The third of these doctrines, for instance, is a dogma of common sense, accepted by philosophers of many different schools as well as by virtually all laymen in all ages. Only the first two of these doctrines, therefore, are in any sense of the word peculiar to the French materialists. Such an analysis of Shelley's early materialism is necessary because the poet discarded the materialism of the *philosophes* some time before he rejected the materialism of common sense.

Shelley's early adherence to French materialism is illustrated by *The Necessity of Atheism* and a number of letters written soon after his expulsion from Oxford. *The Necessity of Atheism,* probably written in colloboration with Hogg,[5] rests squarely on the doctrine that reason and the senses constitute the sole guide to truth. The second doctrine of the French materialists—that spirit can be explained mechanistically—appears more clearly in Shelley's letter to Elizabeth Hitchener, dated June 11, 1811: "What is man without his soul? he is not man. . . . What are vegetables without their vegitative power? stones without their stony? Each of these as much constitutes the essence of men, stones, etc., as much make it to be what it is, as your 'God' does the universe. In this sense I acknowledge a God, but merely as a synonime for the *existing power of existence.* . . ."

But the period during which Shelley adhered to French materialism was probably much briefer than is generally supposed. For instance, neither of the two doctrines just mentioned appears in his works before the pamphlet on atheism, probably written in February, 1811. Both doctrines are apparent, of course, in *A Refutation of Deism* (1814); but since this work is ironical in the sceptical fashion, we must expect the author to introduce many arguments which have nothing to do with his own convictions. In fact, there is considerable evidence indicating that Shelley began to deviate

45

from French materialism even before publishing *Queen Mab* (1813).

One might have foretold that Shelley would soon reject the materialism of the *philosophes* from his letter to Elizabeth Hitchener, dated July 15, 1811: "I recommend reason.—Why? Is it because since I have devoted myself unreservedly to its influencing, I have never felt *happiness?* I find that all pleasure resulting to self is thereby completely annihilated. I am led into this egotism, that you may be clearly aware of the nature of reason, as it affects me." Whatever the purpose of this confession, it marks the beginning of the end of the poet's adherence to French materialism. His next step was to discard the notion that reason is the sole criterion of truth and to embrace certain ideas on the strength of feeling alone. Thus he wrote to Elizabeth Hitchener on October 18, 1811, that "certainly *reason* can never either account for, or prove the truth of, feeling"; and he accepted the truth of two particular conceptions on the basis of an "inward sense": these were "congeniality"—Shelley's term for the affinity he felt with Miss Hitchener—and the doctrine of the soul's immortality. This departure from the basic doctrines of French materialism is reflected in the idyllic relationship assigned to reason and feeling in *Queen Mab,* Canto IX, lines 50-56.

While Shelley rejected French materialism, as we have noted, because it brought him unhappiness, he derived the rational justification for this step from Hume's *Essays,* some of which he had read at Oxford. The poet's brief adherence to French materialism was based on an unqualified acceptance of Locke's theory of knowledge, as indicated by his letter to Elizabeth Hitchener, dated June 11, 1811: "Locke *proves* that there are no innate ideas, that in consequence there can be no innate speculative or practical principles, thus overturning all appeals of *feeling* in favor of Deity, since that feeling must be referable to some origin. There must have been a time when it did not exist; in consequence, a time when it began to exist. Since all ideas are derived from the senses, this *feeling* must have originated from some sensual excitation. . . ." But as the unhappiness resulting to him from this mode of thinking persisted, Shelley recalled or otherwise came upon Hume's qualification of Locke's theory. Hume maintained that "the word *idea,* seems to be commonly taken in a very loose sense, by Locke and others: as standing for any of our perceptions, our sensations and passions, as well as thoughts. Now in this sense, I should desire to know, what can be meant by asserting that self-love, or resentment of injuries, or the passion between the sexes is not innate?"[6] Shelley enthusiastically refers to "Innate Passions" in a letter to Elizabeth Hitchener, dated June 2, 1812. Hume's remark enabled Shelley to combine empiricism with faith in the dictates of the heart, which are innate and not derived from experience or reason.

Drummond was soon to add his influence to Hume's in impressing upon Shelley the fundamental character of the feelings and their significance in human affairs. From Hume and Drummond, and from others influenced by scepticism, Shelley gained insights into the limitations of reason as an instrument not only for the acquisition of knowledge but also for the motivation of human conduct. Scepticism, therefore, led him to place a much higher value upon poetry than upon philosophy. The conclusion of the *Defence of Poetry*—that "poets are the unacknowledged legislators of the world"—is based on premises derived from Hume and Drummond. The same sceptical premises underlie Shelley's abhorrence of didactic poetry and his purpose, as expressed in the Preface to *Prometheus Unbound,* to familiarize "poetical readers with beautiful idealisms of moral excellence; aware that, until the mind can love, and admire, and trust, and hope, and endure, reasoned principles of moral conduct are seeds cast upon the highway of life which the unconscious passenger tramples into dust, although they would bear the harvest of his happiness."

Thus Shelley's sceptical rejection of French materialism was to have far-reaching effects, on both his theory and practice of poetry. No less far-reaching were the effects of his sceptical rejection of common-sense materialism, though this event occurred some years after the former. As Shelley remarks in his essay *On Life,* to reject common-sense materialism involves "a decision against which all our persuasions struggle, and we must be long convicted before we can be convinced that the solid universe of external things is 'such stuff as dreams are made of.'" The apparently contradictory statement that follows this remark is really not contradictory, for it ultimately refers to French materialism and not to common-sense materialism: "The shocking absurdities of the popular philosophy of mind and matter, its fatal consequences in morals, and the violent dogmatism concerning the source of all things, had early conducted me to materialism. This materialism is a seducing system to young and superficial minds. It allows its disciples to talk, and dispenses them from thinking. But I was discontented with such a view of things as it afforded" (VI, 194). Belief in the real existence of external objects was as much a part of the "materialism" which the young poet embraced as of the "popular philosophy" from which he revolted. The term "materialism" in this passage, therefore, can not possibly refer to the materialism of common sense.

Far from being discontented, furthermore, with common-sense materialism, Shelley continued to ridicule efforts to refute it long after his rejection of French materialism. In his Notes to *Queen Mab,* for instance, he refers contemptuously to "the *effluvium* of Boyle and the *crinities* or *nebulae* of

Herschel" (I, 148). On January 6, 1812, Southey wrote to John Rickman regarding Shelley: "He is got to Pantheism already, and in a week more I shall find him a Berkeleyan, for I have put the Minute Philosopher in his hands."[7] But Shelley's reaction to Berkeley, as expressed in a letter to Godwin, dated July 29, 1812, did not fulfill Southey's prediction: "I have read Berkeley, and the perusal of his arguments tended more than anything to convince me that immaterialism, and other words of general usage, deriving all their force from mere predicates in *non,* were invented by the pride of philosophers to conceal their ignorance even from themselves."

The first philosopher to shake the poet's belief in common-sense materialism was probably Hume. This suggestion is supported by the following passage in Shelley's letter to Hogg, dated November 25, 1813: "I have examined Hume's reasonings with respect to the non-existence of external things, and, I confess, they appear to me to follow from the doctrines of Locke. What am I to think of a doctrine that conducts to such a conclusion?" Shelley was to answer his own question in the essay *On Life,* which records his rejection not only of French but also of common-sense materialism. And the philosopher whom Shelley explicitly honors in this essay is Drummond, Hume's principal disciple during Shelley's lifetime.

We may infer that Shelley rejected common-sense materialism on the basis of Hume's theory of cause, as expounded by Hume and Drummond. This theory had played a role in Shelley's thought since his first reading of Hume at Oxford. In the Notes to *Queen Mab,* for instance, the poet writes: "The only idea which we can form of causation is derivable from the constant conjunction of events" (I, 147). Expressed in this form, the theory had contributed to Shelley's anti-religious arguments. But apparently Shelley was unaware, until he re-read Hume in the fall of 1813, that this very theory, with a slight verbal change, casts doubt on the existence not only of an intelligent Creator but also of external objects. In the essay *On Life* Shelley rewords the theory, suggesting his awareness of its application to this new question: "But cause is only a word expressing a certain state of the human mind with regard to the manner in which two thoughts are apprehended to be related to each other" (VI, 197). If our idea of cause is derived from the constant conjunction of *thoughts,* then we may deny the existence of external objects.

Basing his rejection of common-sense materialism on Hume's theory of cause, Shelley was forced, like Hume and Drummond, to reject Berkeley's essential distinction between "real things" and "chimeras." The only valid distinction between these two categories of experience, Shelley remarks in his *Speculations on Metaphysics,* is of a utilitarian character:

> Thoughts, or ideas, or notions, call them what you will, differ from each other, not in kind, but in force. It has commonly been supposed that those distinct thoughts which affect a number of persons, at regular intervals, during the passage of a multiude of other thoughts, which are called *real,* or *external objects,* are totally different in kind from those which affect only a few persons, and which recur at irregular intervals, and are usually more obscure and indistinct, such as hallucinations, dreams, and the ideas of madness. No essential distinction between any one of these ideas, or any class of them, is founded on a correct observation of the nature of things, but merely on a consideration of what thoughts are more invariably subservient to the security and happiness of life.... (VII, 59-60)

Since Shelley followed Hume in rejecting materialism, there is no reason why the poet's immaterialism should agree with Berkeley's. Shelley agrees with Berkeley only where Berkeley agrees with Hume: for instance, in denying the independent existence of phenomena. Shelley's clearest endorsement of this doctrine occurs in the essay *On Life*: "Nothing exists but as it is perceived. The difference is nominal between those two classes of thought, which are vulgarly distinguished by the names of ideas and external objects" (VI, 196). The following apostrophe to *Mont Blanc* expresses this doctrine in different words:

> And what were thou, and earth, and stars, and sea,
> If to the human mind's imaginings
> Silence and solitude were vacancy?

(ll. 142-144)

Another poetic version of the doctrine occurs in these lines from *Hellas*:

> this Whole
> Of suns, and worlds, and men, and beasts, and flowers,
> With all the silent and tempestuous workings
> By which they have been, are, or cease to be,
> Is but a vision;—all that it inherits
> Are motes of a sick eye, bubbles and dreams;
> Thought is its cradle and its grave, no less
> The future and the past are idle shadows
> Of thought's eternal flight—they have no being:
> Nought is but that which feels itself to be.

(ll. 776-785)

It should be noted, however, that to deny the independent existence of phenomena, is merely to express a negative idea: this doctrine confines knowledge to perception; it does not postulate the ideal nature of reality.

Where Hume, however, does not agree with Berkeley, little

agreement will be found between Berkeley and Shelley. The arguments of Hume on which the poet based his rejection of materialism imposed certain restrictions on his idealism—restrictions from which Berkeley was wholly free. After denying cause, for instance, Shelley could not logically assume it to infer, in the manner of Berkeley, that the cause of our perception of phenomena is an infinite mind. "It is said," wrote the poet in *Speculations on Metaphysics,* "that mind produces motion; and it might just as well have been said, that motion produces mind" (VII, 342). Reality for Shelley, as for Hume, would have to remain an unknown quantity—called in *The Triumph of Life* (1. 396) "the realm without a name."

Shelley was still at liberty, of course, to formulate a theory of reality on the uncertain basis of either feeling or probability, and in this manner to pass from the doctrine that denies the independent existence of phenomena to the doctrine that identifies reality with mind. But there is no evidence that he did so. Shelley tends toward the idealism of Plato through a kind of "sceptical solution to doubt," as we shall see in the next chapter; he does not, however, accept Berkeley's concept of reality as mind, even upon the most tentative grounds.

This conclusion is confirmed by the very passages in Shelley which at first appear to contradict it. For instance, after denying the distinction between ideas and external objects in the essay *On Life,* Shelley continues as follows: "Pursuing the same thread of reasoning, the existence of distinct individual minds, similar to that which is employed in now questioning its own nature, is likewise found to be a delusion. The words *I, you, they,* are not signs of any actual difference subsisting between the assemblage of thoughts thus indicated, but are merely marks employed to denote the different modifications of the one mind." But a significant qualification follows this statement, which distinguishes it from the idealism of Berkeley: "Yet, that the basis of all things cannot be, as the popular philosophy, alleges, mind, is sufficiently evident. Mind, as far as we have any experience of its properties, and beyond that experience how vain is argument! cannot create, it can only perceive" (VI, 196-197). In other words, Shelley's "the one mind" appears to be not a metaphysical but a psychological concept, analogous to Jung's well known theory of the "collective unconscious." It refers, at all events, to something less than "the basis of all things."

But if Shelley employed fideism to affirm the existence of a "Spirit of Beauty" in ultimate being, why should he refuse this means of accepting the Berkeleian concept of reality as mind? A plausible conjecture might be that he found in the latter concept some suggestion of an anthropomorphic theology, which he viewed with repugnance (see below, p. 99). There is, in fact, nothing in Shelley's references to Berkeley to indicate that Berkeley ever impressed the poet. Critics have been able to conclude otherwise only by misinterpreting Sir William Drummond, whose "Intellectual Philosophy" Shelley embraced, as Berkeley's disciple (see above, Chapter III).

The concept, therefore, of "thought" and its "elements" in *Hellas,* which appears to echo Berkeley, may not be Berkeleian at all:

> *Thought*
> *Alone, and its quick elements, Will, Passion,*
> *Reason, Imagination, cannot die;*
> *They are what that which they regard appears,*
> *The stuff whence mutability can weave*
> *All that it hath dominion o'er,—worlds, worms,*
> *Empires, and superstitions.*

(11. 795-801)

Since the denial of the independent existence of phenomena is a sceptical as well as a Berkeleian doctrine, and since the concept with which it is here combined probably refers to something less than "the basis of all things," the assumption of Berkeley's influence on such a passage is perhaps unwarranted.

Likewise unwarranted is the belief that the poet's acceptance of immaterialism somehow marked a departure from the political radicalism displayed in *Queen Mab* and other early works. Shelley's political radicalism—which emerged under the influence of Thomas Paine, William Godwin, and the *philosophes*—was well established by 1811.[8] Though Shelley's acceptance of immaterialism occurred somewhat later, it functioned, as we shall see, not in conflict but in harmony with that earlier development of his thought. To recognize such a relationship, however, one must bear in mind what we have just pointed out: that Shelley rejected materialism on the basis of Hume's arguments, not Berkeley's.

Sensible to the limitations of the human mind, the sceptic, it is true, often becomes a conservative in religion and politics, conforming to the customs and beliefs inherited from the past. It is also true that the radical in religion and politics naturally tends toward the worship of "reason" and "nature," which he contrasts to the "superstitions" embodied in the prevailing social order. Despite their admiration for Bayle, whose ironical fideism provided ways of ridiculing the theology of the feudal ages, the *philosophes* seldom manifest any genuine scepticism; their thought logically culminates in the dogmatic materialism of Holbach. But in the early nineteenth century the sceptical rejection of materialism was consistent with the aims of political radicals who were especially opposed to Malthus and the Malthusians.

The first edition of Thomas Robert Maltus' *Essay on the*

Principle of Population (1798), occasioned by Godwin's *The Enquirer*, was intended to demonstrate that the progress of mankind foreseen by Godwin and Condorcet was impossible of attainment. Malthus began by stating his premises: that population, when unchecked, increases in a geometrical ratio; while the means of subsistence, on the other hand, increase only in an arithmetical ratio. The first premise rested on statistics revealing that in certain parts of North America, where the means of subsistence were ample, the population had doubled itself about every twenty to twenty-five years. The second premise was based on plausible speculation: the average produce of England might conceivably be doubled in the next twenty-five years; but one cannot suppose that it could be quadrupled in the second twenty-five years. From these premises Malthus concluded that no extraordinary improvement in the condition of society is possible. Even if a perfect society were once realized, it could not long endure: vice and misery would return in a single generation to check the increase of population beyond the means of subsistence.

Malthus, however, was not satisfied with the *status quo,* although his ideas on reform differed radically from those of previous reformers. His ideas on the subject of reform, presented more fully in the second and later editions of the *Essay,* revealed an unmistakably conservative bias, for they placed the entire burden of alleviating poverty upon the poor themselves. A better condition of society would result, according to Malthus, if the poor were forced to realize the value of moral restraint as a preventive against the evils of excess population. Charitable gifts to the poor, he contended, only increased pauperism. People who brought into the world children whom they could not feed ought to be left to the punishment of nature.

The Malthusian doctrine won numerous converts among

both reactionaries and advocates of equality. Among the former were William Paley, the famous theologian, and Dugald Stewart, the current head of the Common Sense school of philosophy. In his *Natural Theology* (1804) Paley undertook to prove the existence of God from the evidence of design in the universe—particularly in the bodies of animals. The Malthusian ratios provided him with a fresh and timely argument for explaining the presence of evil in creation. What men call evil, Paley held, is ultimately good. If beasts, for instance, did not prey upon one another, the world would soon be filled "with dropping, superannuated, half-starved, helpless, and unhelped animals." Men, of course, do not complain about evils of this kind discoverable in nature; but the same fundamental justification is inherent in the evils about which they do complain: "Mankind will in every country *breed up* to a certain point of distress," and for this "difficulty" and its "attendant circumstances" there is no possible remedy.[9]

In the additions made in 1803 to his *Outlines of Moral Philosophy,* originally published in 1793, Dugald Stewart revealed himself to be, like Paley, a reactionary who early endorsed Malthus. He found Malthus' reasoning to be "just in the main" and was convinced that an unhampered increase in population "does not appear to be a part of the order of Providence." He wondered, therefore, whether the notorious evils connected with the employment of children in the cotton mills "may not have their use in palliating some other disorders of a still more alarming nature." But he salved his conscience by recommending that children's workhouses be restricted to the number required for the orphaned and the destitute.[10]

Malthus, however, won converts among liberals also: these included Samuel Whitbread, Robert Torrens, Richard Carlisle, and Francis Place. Some of these liberals desired a revision of the existing Poor Law in accordance with Malthus' theories—a desire eventually attained in the enactment of the New Poor Law of 1834. Others, however, advocated birth control as a means of checking excess population— a method unacceptable to Malthus, who regarded contraception as a form of vice.

These liberal Malthusians were not so anomalous as might at first appear. Despite his conservative bias, Malthus had much in common with the *philosophes*. Like them, he appealed to reason and the laws of nature. No French materialist gave greater emphasis than he to the physical basis of moral codes. Furthermore, he admitted the beauty of the future society conceived by Godwin and Condorcet. The main difference between Malthus and the perfectibilitarians was a simple one: they felt that nature had put practically no limits on human hopes, while he argued that nature had laid insurmountable obstacles across the path of progress. In effect, therefore, Malthusianism constituted an ironical conclusion to the Age of Reason, glorified by the *philosophes*—a conclusion in which a conservative had confounded the radicals by erecting a reactionary system of thought upon their axioms. This ironical state of affairs was partly responsible for the increasingly sceptical and anti-materialistic tendencies in William Godwin after 1798.

The early William Godwin, that is, the author of *Political Justice* (1793), tended toward a dogmatism like that of the French materialists. Among speculations productive of mischief, he asserted, was the theory "that passion is not to be conquered by reason, but by bringing some other passion into contention with it." "Man," he held, "is a rational being." Admitting absolute certainty to be unattainable, he pointed out that human science is attended with various degrees of probability, "and to know the exact quantity of probability which I ought to ascribe to any proposition, may be said in a sense to be the possession of certain knowledge." "Nor will he," Godwin continued, "who is sufficiently conversant with the science of intellect, be hasty in assigning the bounds of our capacity."[11]

But after the appearance of Malthus' *Essay* in 1798, Godwin inclined more and more toward scepticsim in philosophy. Replying to Malthus in 1801, Godwin wrote: "Every impartial person who knows me, or has attentively considered my writings, will acknowledge that it is the fault of my character, rather to be too sceptical, than to incline too much to play the dogmatist. I was by no means assured of the truth of my own system."[12] Eight years later he remarked that he was "more inclined to the opinion of the immaterialists, than of the materialists."[13] His letter to Shelley, dated December 10, 1812, offers advice that might have come from Drummond: "The light in which I should wish every man . . . to consider the study of history, is a means of becoming acquainted with whatever of noble, useful, generous, and admirable, human nature is capable of designing and performing. To see all this illustrated by examples carrying it directly into act, is, perhaps, superior to all the theories and speculations that can possibly be formed."[14]

The best record of Godwin's scepticism, however, is to be found in his essay "Of Astronomy," included in his *Thoughts on Man*. Though this book did not appear until 1831, Godwin had probably reached the ideas expressed in it before his first meeting with Shelley in the fall of 1812.[15] Godwin begins his essay with a brief history of the metaphysics attacked by the Common Sense school—how Berkeley had taught many to doubt the existence of matter, how "later theorists" arrived at the conclusion that each of us may "be the only thing that exists, an entire universe to ourselves." He then comments upon the limitations of the human mind:

> . . . we know what passes in the theatre of the mind; but we cannot be said absolutely to know anything more. In our speculations upon actual existences we are not only subject to the disadvantages which arise from the limited nature of our faculties, and the errors which may creep upon us in the process. We are further exposed to the operation of the unevenness and irregularities that perpetually occur in external nature, the imperfections of our senses and the instruments we contruct to assist our observations, and the discrepancy which we frequently detect between the actual nature of things about us and our impressions respecting them.

As an example of an erroneous theory resulting from such natural limitations of the human mind, Godwin cites the arithmetical and geometrical ratios "set up in political economy by the celebrated Mr. Malthus."[16]

Shelley's sceptical rejection of materialism, as we have already noted, resulted from the needs of his own character and from reason. Nevertheless, he was, as we shall see, fully aware of the opposition between his sceptical rejection of materialism and the dogmatism of the Malthusians. In a letter to Godwin, dated July 29, 1812, Shelley expressed the view that "the doctrine which affirms that there is no such thing as matter, and that which affirms that all is matter, appear to me, perfectly indifferent in the question between benevolence and self-love." But in the essay *On Life,* written some years later, he had changed his mind on this point, maintaining that only the "Intellectual Philosophy" is compatible with the Miltonic view of man as a being of high aspirations (VI, 194). The dogmatism of the Malthusians possibly convinced Shelley that a sceptical attitude served best in conducting man "To fear himself, and love all humankind."[17]

The poet probably first encountered Malthusianism in the works of William Paley and Dugald Stewart. Stewart was perhaps one of the "Scotch metaphysicians of inferior ability" whom Hogg and he had read at Oxford.[18] A little later, according to Hogg (I, 184-185), Sir Timothy employed Paley in a futile attempt to convert Shelley to Christianity. In the notes to *A Refutation of Deism* the poet refers to both Paley's *Natural Theology* and Stewart's *Outlines of Moral Philosophy* (VI, 45). These two works present the more disagreeable aspects of Malthusianism as clearly as possible. Perhaps Shelley saw in them illustrations of the sceptic's contention that reason in practice is the slave of the passions, degenerating into selfish sophistry when not motivated by charity and love.

At all events the dogmatism of the Malthusians may help us to understand, by way of contrast, the poet's admiration for Drummond, who had tried to revive the scepticism of Hume. In the Preface to *The Revolt of Islam* Shelley wrote: "Metaphysics, and enquiries into moral and political sciences, have become little else than vain attempts to revive exploded superstitions, or sophisms like those of Mr. Malthus, calculated to lull the oppressors of mankind into a security of everlasting triumph." To this condemnation of contemporary thought, he added the following qualifying note: "I ought to except Sir W. Drummond's 'Academical Questions'; a volume of very acute and powerful metaphysical criticism."

But Shelley's most significant contrast between Malthusian dogmatism and scepticism occurs in *Prometheus Unbound*. Jupiter's flattering but dogmatic and false assumptions regarding ultimate reality appear in his vision of the "fatal child," who probably symbolizes the Malthusian doctrine.[19] In contrast to this creature of the tyrant's intoxicated fancy stands

Demogorgon, the inconceivable ultimate reality of scepticism. As Panthea describes him, Demogorgon is amorphous:

> *I see a mighty darkness*
> *Filling the seat of power, and rays of gloom*
> *Dart round, as light from the meridian sun,*
> *Ungazed upon and shapeless; neither limb,*
> *Nor form, nor outline; yet we feel it is*
> *A living Spirit.*

(II, iv, 2-7)

To Asia's questions regarding ultimate reality, Demogorgon replies like a sceptic:

> *If the abysm*
> *Could vomit forth its secrets. But a voice*
> *Is wanting, the deep truth is imageless. . . .*
> (II, iv, 114-116)

Shelley, then, rejected materialism on the basis of sceptical arguments traceable mainly to Hume. Furthermore, the poet's sceptical rejection of materialism, far from being inconsistent with his political radicalism, confirmed his opposition to its most dangerous contemporary foes. There now remains the question of the relationship between Shelley's immaterialism and his necessarianism. Many of the poet's critics have concluded that when he abandoned materialism, he also discarded or was logically bound to discard the doctrine of Necessity.

There is, perhaps, a theoretical conflict between Shelley's necessarianism and his passion for reforming the world, on the ground that any form of determinism reduces man to the status of a passive and irresponsible agent. Nevertheless, some of the world's greatest reformers—St. Augustine, John Calvin, Karl Marx—have been determinists of one kind or another. As Crane Brinton remarks, "these firm believers in the inability of human effort to *change* anything were among the most ardent workers toward getting men to change their behavior."[20] This paradox is not difficult to explain: the reformer's zeal is not weakened but strengthened if the reformer feels it to be the expression of divine or cosmic power. Determinism and reform, therefore, are compatible in practice, although they may not seem to be so in theory.

But whatever theoretical antithesis may exist between determinism and reform, there can be no logical conflict between determinism and immaterialism. The idea of necessary connection is as applicable to a universe conceived as thought as to one conceived as matter. The view, therefore, that Shelley, upon becoming an immaterialist, was logically bound to discard his doctrine of Necessity must rest on the assumption that he derived his doctrine of Necessity from materialist philosophers. It is obvious that materialism cannot be reconciled with immaterialism; consequently if Shelley derived his doctrine of Necessity from the materialist Holbach, he would be chargeable with a fundamental confusion.

But the truth, strange as it might at first appear, is that Shelley's idea of Necessity is traceable not to materialism but to scepticism, being derived, directly and indirectly, from Hume. Hume's concept of Necessity, it will be recalled, is conditional, tentative, and philosophically ironical. All we know of causation is the constant conjunction of objects in the external world or of ideas in our own mind. If we ascribe the fiction of necessary connection to the former type of sequence, we are logically bound to ascribe it to the latter kind also, thus rejecting the freedom of the will (see above, pp. 21-22). The same argument, it will be recalled, occurs in Sir William Drummond (see above, p. 31). The young Shelley's idea of Necessity, as stated in the Notes to *Queen Mab* (1813), is similarly based on Hume's theory of causation: "The idea of necessity is obtained by our experience of the connection between objects, the uniformity of the operations of nature, the constant conjunction of similar events, and the consequent inference of one from the other" (I, 144). The young Shelley, of course, wrote *Queen Mab* before he had come under the full impact of the sceptical tradition: unlike Hume and Drummond, therefore, the young poet does not emphasize the fictional character of Necessity. Nevertheless, his concept is derived, directly or indirectly, from Hume.

The true source of Shelley's idea of Necessity was demonstrated in a recent article by Frank B. Evans, who concluded that "Godwin borrowed his account of necessity from Hume, and Shelley derived his doctrine of necessity from Hume and Godwin." But this critic, somewhat oddly, contradicts the essence of his own conclusion: "There is none of Hume's scepticism, however, in Godwin and Shelley. A hardened dogmatism takes its place. . . . Shelley and Godwin mean that the necessity of causation inheres in the structure of reality."[21] These remarks may be partially valid in regard to the doctrine of Necessity contained in the Notes to *Queen Mab*—which is the only expression of Shelley's doctrine considered by Mr. Evans; but the remarks hardly apply to the poet in his maturity.

To the mature Shelley, as to Hume, Necessity is fundamentally an unknown power. In *On a Future State* the poet refers to it as "the mysterious principle that regulates the proceedings of the universe" (VI, 206). Several references to this "mysterious principle" occur in *Mont Blanc*, a key work to the understanding of the mature poet's philosophy:

> *awful scene,*
> *Where Power in likeness of the Arve comes down*
> *From the ice-gulfs that gird his secret throne . . .*
>
> (ll. 15-17)

> *Power dwells apart in its tranquility,*
> *Remote, serene, and inaccessible. . . .*
>
> (11. 96-97)

> *The secret Strength of things*
> *Which governs thought, and to the infinite dome*
> *Of Heaven is as a law . . .*
>
> (11. 139-141)

If Necessity has a "secret throne," if it is "inaccessible," if it represents the "secret Strength of things," the poet is certainly suggesting that it is an unknown power; and to assert the unknowability of Necessity is to express scepticism and not a "hardened dogmatism."

Scepticism, however, often leads to some kind of faith. In Shelley's case, it led to faith in the essential soundness of his already active passion for reforming the world. In accordance with this faith, therefore, he held that Necessity, though an unknown power, must operate in favor of the perfectibilitarians. The following lines in *Mont Blanc* express this relationship between the sceptic's "awful doubt" (a sense of the mystery of Necessity) [22] and his "faith so mild" (a feeling that Necessity assures the progress of mankind) :

> *The wilderness has a mysterious tongue*
> *Which teaches awful doubt, or faith so mild,*
> *So solemn, so serene, that man may be,*
> *But for such faith,[23] with nature reconciled;*
> *Thou hast a voice, great Mountain, to repeal*
> *Large codes of fraud and woe; not understood*
> *By all, but which the wise, and great, and good*
> *Interpret, or make felt, or deeply feel.*
>
> (11. 76-83)

Thus, through faith, the "secret Strength of things" is converted into a "voice" capable of repealing "Large codes of fraud and woe." These two aspects of Shelley's doctrine of Necessity are perfectly fused in the conception of Demogorgon, the amorphous and mysterious being who effects the triumph of Prometheus over Jupiter.

But Shelley recognized that the unknown power inherent in reality could not be interpreted fully in accordance with his own aspirations. The ascription of intelligence to reality conflicted with one of the poet's firmest convictions. Furthermore, Shelley was quite aware of the fact that the "secret Strength of things" must govern what we call evil as well as what we call good. Despite, therefore, his faith in the perfectibilitarian tendency of Necessity, he avoids ascribing to it either intelligence or a consciously benevolent purpose. In *The Revolt of Islam,* for instance, Necessity is described as a "sightless" being, who joins evil to evil as well as good to good:

> One comes behind,
> Who aye the future to the past will bind—
> Necessity, whose sightless strength forever
> Evil with evil, good with good must wind
> In bands of union, which no power may sever:
> They must bring forth their kind, and be divided never.

(IX, xxii)

And in the Prologue to *Hellas* Satan refers to "Destiny" as

> thou Vicegerent of my will, no less
> Than of the Father's . . .

(11. 142-143)

Once we recognize the sceptical quality of Shelley's idea of Necessity, the conclusion of *Mont Blanc* is seen to be not anti-climactic but climactic:

And what were thou, and earth, and stars, and sea,
If to the human mind's imaginings
Silence and solitude were vacancy?

(11. 142-144)

These lines do not express, as Mr. Kapstein believes (see above, p. 43), a shift of attitude toward Necessity which disrupts the unity of the poem. Rather the lines bring to a suitable climax the scepticism pervading *Mont Blanc* as a whole: that Necessity is an unknown power and any conception of it must be a fiction, a creation of the imagination.

To summarize: Shelley cannot be considered a confused Berkeleian, for his rejection of materialism was based on Hume's arguments, not Berkeley's. This acceptance of immaterialism on sceptical grounds involves, in Shelley's case, no rejection of the revolutionary zeal of the French materialists; it involves only a rejection of their dogmatic materialism, which contemporary reactionaries had adapted, with great success, to their own purposes. Furthermore, Shelley's mature doctrine of Necessity is not an incongruous vestige of his juvenile materialism, being derived, directly and indirectly, from the same source as his immaterialism—the philosophy of scepticism. The poet's necessarianism and immaterialism, accordingly, represent not contradictory ontologies but compatible aspects of a fundamentally sceptical philosophy joined to a perfectibilitarian faith. This conclusion, if sound, is of some importance: it reduces to a myth the incredible spectacle of a major English poet, justly praised by some critics for his grasp of speculative thought, attempting to combine Holbach's materialist determinism with Berkeley's view of the spiritual nature of reality.

V

SCEPTICISM AND PLATONISM

SHELLEY "felt the radiance and breathed the air of Plato's genius," said Edward Dowden, "as though he were himself a scholar in the garden at Colonus."[1] But another nineteenth-century critic, Walter Bagehot, felt that "there is in Shelley none of that unceasing reference to ethical consciousness and ethical religion which has for centuries placed Plato first among the preparatory preceptors of Christianity."[2] Early twentieth-century critics likewise disagreed sharply regarding Shelley's Platonism. Treating the subject more fully and systematically than had any of her predecessors, Lillian Winstanley arrived at the following conclusion: "Shelley was one of those men who are, by temperament, born Platonists, and it may be surmised that, had he never read a line of Greek or even heard of Plato, except by indirect tradition only, his work would still show a certain number of affinities. Natural resemblance and close study, taken together, have resulted in

saturating his whole work with Platonic thought. . . ."[3]
Combining a similar verdict with considerations minimized
by Lillian Winstanley, C. H. Hereford declared three years
later: "Under forms of thought derived from the atheist and
materialist Godwin, Shelley has given in *Prometheus Unbound,* magnificient expression to the faith of Plato and of
Christ."[4] Hereford's remark drew this comment from Paul
Elmer More: "The faith of Plato and of Christ! Shall I
confess that to meet with such words in such a place is to be
overborne with the futility of writing at all."[5]

Faced with the question whether Shelley was a Platonist
or a pseudo-Platonist, recent critics have avoided taking ex-
treme positions and have sought, in various ways, the reaching
of a compromise. Carl Grabo, for instance, discovers two
factors that tended to differentiate Shelley's Platonism from
Plato: the influence of the Neoplatonists and the desire to
reconcile idealism with the speculations of current science.[6]
Another recent critic, Ellsworth Barnard, fully concedes the
existence of fundamental differences between Shelley's and
Plato's concepts of Beauty; but he argues that Shelley's concept may be as adequate as Plato's "to the actual needs of men
in their struggle toward a higher state of existence than they
have yet attained."[7] Finally, James A. Notopoulos suggests
that Shelley was not an expounder of Plato's philosophy but a
"natural" Platonist, and that "those who condemn Shelley
as a pseudo-Platonist confuse natural Platonism with Plato's
expression of it."[8]

If Shelley did not expound the philosophy of Plato, perhaps the philosophy that he did expound helped to determine
the special character of his Platonism. This idea is no doubt
implied in Mr. Grabo's theory that the Neoplatonists influenced Shelley's Platonism. The philosophy, however, that
Shelley expounded was not that of Plotinus and Porphyry,[9]

but, as I have tried to show, that of Hume and Drummond. What the present chapter will attempt to suggest is that scepticism prepared the way for Shelley's acceptance of Plato and at the same time rendered inevitable his basic divergence from Plato.

The sceptical tradition prepared the way for Shelley's acceptance of Plato by resolving the objection to Plato held by the *philosophes* and by depicting Plato as a kind of sceptic himself—or as, at least, a forerunner of scepticism.

The attitude of the eighteenth century toward Plato was largely one of disparagement, characteristic of which was Bolingbroke's remark that Plato was "the father of philosophical lying." Owing to the increasing activity of Platonic scholars, this unappreciative point of view was questioned in the last forty years of the century.[10] Little influenced, however, by this revival of Platonic scholarship, the *philosophes* continued to regard Plato as a mere poetic "dreamer" (see Notopoulos, 137 ff.), not to be taken seriously by modern philosophers. Shelley's first reference to Plato (I, 33-37), written before he had come under the influence of the *philosophes* (January, 1810), is quite free of any adverse criticism:

> *Your writings may then with old Socrates vie,*
> *May on the same shelf with Demosthenes lie,*
> *May as Junius be sharp, or as Plato be sage. . . .*

In the Notes to *Queen Mab* (1813), however, the poet employed the phrase "the reveries of Plato" (VII, 135-136) in a context clearly suggesting that he no longer regarded Plato as "sage," but had come to see him after the fashion of the *philosophes* as a kind of poetic "dreamer." From this point of view regarding Plato Shelley was liberated, and liberated completely, by the influence upon him of the sceptical tradition. Although even the mature poet's unquestionable admiration for Plato is qualified by the admission of certain defects, that admission neither includes nor suggests the main charge directed against Plato by the *philosophes*.

Illustrative of the mature Shelley's attitude toward Plato is the Preface to his translation of *The Symposium*. The poet praises Plato's "view into the nature of mind and existence" as "profound" and "remarkable intuitions." On the other hand, he implies that he is not in complete agreement with Plato's views on "the government of the world" and "the elementary laws of moral action"; and he concedes, furthermore, that the dialogues are "stained by puerile sophisms" (VII, 161). This last charge contains the main substance of the mature poet's adverse criticism of the Greek philosopher. That it expresses a settled opinion, and not an echo of an earlier attitude, is indicated by its recurrence, as we shall see, in diverse references to Plato in the mature Shelley.

A comparison of this charge against Plato with that which the young Shelley had derived from the *philosophes* reveals a categorical difference: the mature poet objects to Plato's "sophisms," whereas the young poet had objected to his "reveries." The term "reveries" refers mainly to the Platonic myths and parables. The term "sophisms," however, refers not to the Platonic myths, but to the results of a mode of reasoning. A mode of reasoning that sometimes led Plato to utter what might conceivably impress one as "puerile sophisms" was the "induction of dialectic," which Diogenes Laertius explains as follows: "For instance, the question put is whether the soul is immortal, and whether the living come back from the dead. And this is proved in the dialogue *On the Soul* by means of a general proposition, that opposites proceed from opposites. And the general proposition itself is established by means of certain propositions which are particular, as that sleep comes from waking and *vice versa*, the greater from the less and *vice versa*" (iii. 55).

A consideration of the specific "sophisms" to which Shelley refers clearly indicates that they were the results of Plato's "induction of dialectic." To Socrates' question in the *Ion* (535) whether an actor is not mad who, with no one despoiling him or wronging him, "appears weeping or panic-stricken in the presence of more than twenty thousand friendly faces," Shelley replies in a note: "A sophism here. Tears did not indicate grief or horror. . . ." The error in this instance lies in a "particular proposition" of the "induction of dialectic." In his *On A Passage in Crito,* on the other hand, Shelley apparently objects to a "general proposition," for, after rewriting Socrates' account of a good citizen's duty to obey the laws of his country, the poet remarks: "Such are the arguments, which overturn the sophism placed in the mouth of Socrates by Plato" (VII, 265). Elsewhere Shelley's reference to a specific Platonic sophism recalls one of the examples cited by Diogenes Laertius in his explanation of the "induction of dialectic"—that the greater comes from the less and vice versa: "Perhaps all discontent with the *less* (to use a Platonic sophism) supposes the sense of a just claim to the *greater*" (X, 371).

But while the mature Shelley not infrequently finds fault with the results of Plato's "induction of dialectic," he still exhibits an extraordinary admiration for the Greek philosopher. No contradiction is involved here, for Shelley did not regard Plato as primarily a "mere reasoner," to be judged only by the standards of logic. In *A Defence of Poetry,* for instance, he writes: "Plato was essentially a poet—the truth and splendour of his imagery, and the melody of his language, is the most intense that it is possible to conceive" (VII, 114).

In other words, Shelley came to set the highest value upon those very elements in the Platonic philosophy which in his youth, under the influence of the *philosophes,* he had contemptuously referred to as "the reveries of Plato."

In regarding Plato as essentially a poet, the mature Shelley was not partially following the example of the *philosophes,* as might at first appear; he was following the example of the sceptics. "Plato," said Montaigne, "is but a loose poet."[13] The *philosophes* may sometimes describe Plato in almost the same words. But between Montaigne's meaning and that of the *philosophes* there lies a basic and significant difference. Montaigne was defining philosophy, not ridiculing Plato, when he called the Greek philosopher a poet. As a sceptic, he esteemed the "poetry" in Plato as the reaction of human nature to the unknown and unknowable. The *philosophes,* on the other hand, meant that Plato lacked their solidity of thought and knowledge. As dogmatists, they had no intention whatever of identifying metaphysics with poetry. For a time the young Shelley followed the view of the *philosophes*; but as he enlarged his acquaintance with the sceptical tradition, he discarded their view for that of Montaigne, whom he read in the fall of 1816.[14]

The mature Shelley's revaluation of Plato may have owed something to another aspect of the sceptical tradition, pertaining not to the positive but to the negative side of the Greek philosopher's thought: I allude to the tendency among sceptics to claim Plato as an intellectual ancestor. Plato, of course, is not a sceptic. Socrates' claim of ignorance was largely ironic; his inconclusiveness in some of the dialogues resulted from his maieutic method, not from doubt and uncertainty. Socrates' disavowal of scepticism is clearly expressed in the *Meno,* 86: "Some things I have said of which I am not altogether confident. But that we shall be better and braver and less helpless if we think that we ought to enquire, than we should have been if we indulged in the idle fancy that there was no knowing and no use in seeking to know what we do not know;— that is a theme upon which I am ready to fight, in word and deed, to the utmost of my power."

Nevertheless, there have been sceptics in both ancient and modern times who have interpreted Plato as a sceptic rather than a dogmatist. Cicero, for instance, agreed with Philo of Larissa that the school of Plato and the New Acadamy were not two schools of thought but one (*Academica* i. 13). Disagreeing with Cicero regarding the classification of Plato, Varro granted, however, that Socrates was a sceptic, whose method was "to affirm nothing himself but to refute others, to assert that he knows nothing but the fact of his own ignorance" (*Academica* i. 16). Diogenes Laertius suggested a compromise on the issue: "where he has a firm grasp Plato expounds his own view and refutes the false one, but, if the subject is obscure, he suspends judgment" (iii. 51-52). Montaigne, however, returned to the position of Cicero: "They [Socrates and Plato] will not make open profession of ignorance, and the imbecillitie of mans reason, because they will not make children afraid: But they manifestly declare the same unto us under the show of a troubled Science and unconstant learning" (II, 255-256).

Though in a degree erroneous, this interpretation of Plato as a sceptic has enjoyed a respectable history; and it quite possibly contributed to the re-awakening of Shelley's interest in Platonism by relating Plato to a philosophical point of view that the poet himself had embraced. It is generally agreed that the renascence of Shelley's Platonism began at Marlow in 1817. By that date Shelley had virtually completed his study of the sceptical tradition—a study that had begun in earnest in the fall of 1813. By 1817, therefore, Shelley was quite familiar with the interpretation of Plato as a sceptic. That the poet endorsed this interpretation is suggested by his remark to Trelawny in 1822: "With regard to the great question, the System of the Universe, I have no curiosity on the subject. I am content to see no farther into futurity than Plato and Bacon."[15]

Scepticism, however, not only prepared the way for Shelley's acceptance of Plato but also inevitably determined his basic divergence from Plato. While both Shelley and Plato exhibit tendencies often vaguely referred to as "transcendental," the nature of these tendencies is quite different in the two men. A brief comparison of the epistemological views of each with those of the strict transcendentalists may help to clarify this underlying difference.

Strict transcendentalism had its origin in Kant's effort to refute Hume. Kant presented two ways by which to surmount the obstacles to knowledge set up by the British sceptic. First, he held that such categories as time, space, and causality are not empirical concepts as Hume maintained but *a priori* concepts. Secondly, he pointed out that just as the "understanding" makes use of such *a priori* concepts in science, so "pure reason" employs the ideas of soul, universe, and God in metaphysics. Kant did not, however, assign to knowledge based on "pure reason" the certitude that he assigned to knowledge based on the "understanding"; it was possible, according to his principles, to know phenomena but not things-in-themselves or reality. But Kant's successors—Fichte, Schelling, and Hegel—rejected this reservation;[16] while English and American writers who came under the direct or indirect influence of the German idealists seized upon Kant's distinction to sanction free intuitive thinking, by exalting "pure reason" and abasing the "understanding."

Plato's epistemology is both like and unlike that of the strict transcendentalists. Like them, Plato is no empiricist, for his doctrine of reminiscence amply recognizes the possibility of *a priori* knowledge. Socrates illustrates his view "that all knowledge is but recollection" by eliciting from a Greek slave of Meno's, previously ignorant of geometry, the proof of one of Euclid's theorems (*Meno* 81-85). To the extent that it rests on legends, particularly on the legend of the soul's pre-existence, the doctrine of reminiscence has, perhaps, the quality of a myth—the kind of myth to which Plato resorted when his subject was obscure. Aside from its mythical quality, however, the doctrine suggests the theory of innate ideas. At all events Plato seriously adhered to the view that all knowledge is latent in the mind, and that such knowledge can be recovered after we become conscious of our ignorance.

Since Plato held that all knowledge is latent in the mind, he was free, like the strict transcendentalists, to pass from the world of becoming to the world of being; to seek not the knowledge of phenomena but "that other sort of knowledge which reason herself attains by the power of dialectic, using hypotheses not as first principles but only as hypotheses—that is to say, as steps and points of departure into a world which is above hypotheses, in order that she may soar beyond them to the first principle of the whole; and clinging to this and then to that which depends on this, by successive steps she descends again without the aid of any sensible object, from ideas through ideas, and in ideas she ends" (*Republic* 511). But as this passage suggests, his method was dialectical rather than intuitive. Innocent of the Kantian distinction, he could not, like Emerson, for instance, ignore logic because he was employing "pure reason."

Reared in the empirical tradition of British philosophy, Shelley never seriously considered the possibility of *a priori* knowledge, which constitutes so essential a feature of strict transcendentalism and Platonism. While a student at Oxford in the winter of 1810-1811, he was converted by Locke to the doctrine that all knowledge is derived ultimately from experience—a doctrine he never abandoned, although he accepted the slight modification of it involved in Hume's theory of innate passions (see above, p. 47). Shelley also embraced Hume's empirical concept of cause—a concept that played a major role in the poet's rejection of materialism for scepticism. His subsequent admiration for Plato, being an effect, as we have seen, of this development, can hardly be used as evidence of a change in his epistemological views. Nor is there any reason for suspecting that the poet's empiricism was ever undermined by the influence of strict transcendentalism. His letter to Clair Clairmont, dated February 18, 1821, suggests modesty and tact rather than approval of his correspondent's interest in German philosophy. Shelley, like Sir William Drummond, was hostile rather than friendly toward Kant and his "disciples," as the following passage in *Peter Bell the Third* makes abundantly clear:

> *The Devil then sent to Leipsic fair,*
> *   For Born's translation of Kant's Book;*
> *A world of words, tail foremost, where*
> *Right—wrong—false—true—and foul—and fair,*
> *   As in a lottery-wheel are shook.*
>
> *Five thousand crammed octavo pages*
> *   Of German psychologies,—he*
> *Who his* furor verborum *assuages*
> *Thereon, deserves just seven months' wages*
> *   More than will e'er be due to me.*

> *I looked on them nine several days,*
>   *And then I saw that they were bad;*
> *A friend, too, spoke in their dispraise,—*
> *He never read them;—with amaze*
>   *I found Sir William Drummond had.*
>
> (Part the Sixth, 11. 61-75)

One might insist that despite this hostility in theory, Shelley in practice resembles the strict transcendentalists; for in dealing with the great and eternal questions, he turns from reason to the imagination, exactly as they turn from the "understanding" to "pure reason." But this affinity has perhaps been overemphasized, its limitations ignored. To strict transcendentalists like Coleridge and Emerson, "pure reason" is a superior form of thinking and not a non-rational source of provisional assent. Wordsworth illustrates this point in his well known definition of the imagination as "reason in her most exalted mood"—a view with which most strict transcendentalists would agree. Never accepting, however, the distinction betwen a lower and a higher rational faculty, Shelley avoids such confounding of imagination with reason.[17] In conceiving of what lies beyond phenomena, he resorts to the sceptic's faith or the sceptic's doctrine of probability. He does not make dogmatical assertions about unknowable things but expresses tentative feelings about things recognized as unknowable.

How Shelley's Humean theory of knowledge influenced his apprehension of ultimate being is illustrated by his Platonism. It is generally agreed that the main feature of Shelley's Platonism is his pursuit of Beauty. The major differences between his pursuit of Beauty and Plato's are well known. While Plato ascends progressively from particular beauties to Beauty, Shelley tends to reverse this process and to seek Beauty in its earthly manifestations. Furthermore, while Plato seeks Beauty through dialectic, Shelley apprehends it only through imagination and feeling. What we are concerned with attempting to demonstrate is that these differences between the two men were the direct result of their dissimilar theories of knowledge. This hypothesis may be tested by examining the development of their concepts of Beauty.

It is quite possible, as William Temple maintained, that in both Plato's case and Shelley's the concept of Beauty had its genesis in a mystical experience. In the *Symposium,* this critic held, Plato "prepares us for a doctrine that is not only quite unsocratic, but has about it the dignity of a religious dogma. It is the prophetess who speaks, but the experience described is Plato's. . . . The language of initiation is freely used; the prophetess is afraid Socrates may not be able to follow τὰ τέλεα καὶ ἐποπτικά, in whose interest all other love exists."[18] To proceed aright, according to Diotima, a person should begin in his youth to visit beautiful forms; if properly guided by his instructor, the youth will love but one such form, out of which he will create fair thoughts, until he perceives "that the beauty of one form is akin to the beauty of another" and "that the beauty in every form is one and the same." In the next stage he will discover "that the beauty of mind is more honourable than the beauty of the outward form," a realization enabling him to see the beauty of institutions, laws, sciences; until at last the vision is revealed to him of "beauty absolute, separate, simple, and everlasting, which without diminution and without increase, or any change, is imparted to the evergrowing and perishing beauties of all other things" (*Symposium* 210-211).

That Shelley's concept of Beauty owed its genesis to a mystical experience is suggested by the following passage in the *Hymn to Intellectual Beauty*:

While yet a boy I sought for ghosts, and sped
  Thro' many a listening chamber, cave, and ruin,
  And starlight wood, with fearful steps pursuing
Hopes of high talk with the departed dead.
I called on poisonous names with which our youth is fed:
  I was not heard: I saw them not:
  When musing deeply on the lot
Of life, at that sweet time when woods are wooing
  All vital things that wake to bring
  News of birds and blossoming,
  Sudden, thy shadow fell on me;
I shrieked, and clasped my hands in extacy!

(11. 49-60)

Shelley's account of his experience makes no mention of an "instructor"; nor does it employ the "language of initiation." Nevertheless, it is analogous to Plato's in suggesting the mystical origin of the same philosophical concept.

But while Plato and Shelley may have owed the genesis of their vision to similar mystical experiences, they had to relate their concepts of Beauty to quite dissimilar theories of knowledge; and this difference in the nature of their problems led to a considerable difference in their solutions. In his early dialogues, including the *Meno,* Plato had treated the Ideas as being immanent in particular things. His first clear assertion of the transcendence of Beauty occurs in the mystical passage ascribed to Diotima in the *Symposium.* It is in the next dialogue, the *Phaedo,* that Plato for the first time relates his concept of Beauty to his theory of knowledge— the theory that all knowledge is recollection: "Then may we not say, Simmias, that if, as we are always repeating, there is an absolute beauty, and goodness, and an absolute essense of all things; and if to this, which is now discovered to have existed

79

in our former state, we refer all our sensations, and with this compare them, finding these ideas to be pre-existent and our inborn possession—then our souls must have had a prior existence, but if not, then there would be no force in the argument" (76).

By relating the Ideas to his doctrine of reminiscence, Plato was able to convert the concept of Beauty, previously but the expression of a mystical experience, into a metaphysical doctrine, a theory of reality. Apart from the world of phenomena, which is subject to the Heracleitean flux, exist, Plato now came to hold on rational grounds, certain perfect and immutable forms. Though the soul cannot perfectly apprehend these essences so long as it is chained to the body, the philosopher in considerable measure escapes this limitation, since he spends his life in the pursuit of death, that is, in emancipating the soul from the body's domination and control (*Phaedo* 63-69). Accordingly, Plato was led to disparage poets and to glorify philosophers, on the ground that only the latter seek the true objects of knowledge, not the perishing forms and shadows of becoming, apprehended by the senses and the feelings, but the fixed and eternal patterns of being, discoverable only by the reason (*Republic* 597-608).

But while Plato's theory of knowledge enabled him to convert Beauty into a metaphysical concept based on reason, Shelley's theory of knowledge prevented him from following a similar course. Shelley's theory of knowledge confined the scope of reason to that prescribed by Hume's theory of causation. Within these limits only science and a negative metaphysics were possible. In the poet's own words, "metaphysical science" is to be treated "as a source of negative truth" (VII, 71). Philosophy, in other words, can destroy superstition, disprove the theory of innate ideas, invalidate the assumption of the efficacy of causes; but it can shed no light whatever on the nature of ultimate reality. Curiosity about ultimate being is therefore futile. In a letter to Thomas Medwin, dated August 22, 1821, Shelley wrote: "What were the speculations which you say disturbed you? My mind is at peace respecting nothing so much as the constitution and mysteries of the great system of things;—my curiosity on the point never amounts to solicitude." Shelley's problem, therefore, was to relate his mystical experience of Beauty, not to Plato's doctrine of reminiscence, but to Hume's theory of knowledge.

Shelley's first effort in poetry to adjust his concept of Beauty to a sceptical theory of knowledge appears in *Alastor* (1815). We are told in the Preface to this poem that the hero "images to himself the Being whom he loves" and then "seeks in vain for the prototype of his conception." The misinterpretation of these two points in the Preface has done much to make *Alastor* seem confused to its critics. As Evan K. Gibson has recently pointed out, the "Being" imaged by the hero is "a creation of his own mind and not, as some writers have stated, a vision sent to him by some outside agency"; and the "prototype" he seeks is not "a copy of the vision in the actual world" but "the pattern or original of the vision itself," that is, absolute Beauty. The hero's quest during his life proves futile; and whether he finds what he seeks after his death is a question to which Shelley gives no clear and definite answer.[20] In other words, Shelley implies in *Alastor* that Beauty, so far as we know, has no objective existence. The tragedy of the hero of *Alastor* lies in his failure to realize this conviction of his creator. Instead of looking for the likeness of his vision in a human maiden, the hero of *Alastor* vainly seeks to apprehend its pattern in ultimate reality.

Likewise adapted to a sceptical theory of knowledge is the concept described in *Hymn to Intellectual Beauty* (1816).

Man, according to the poet, is confronted by certain un-answerable questions:

No voice from some sublimer world hath ever
To sage or poet these responses given:
Therefore the name of Demon, Ghost, and Heaven,
Remain the records of their vain endeavour:
Frail spells, whose uttered charm might not avail to sever,
From all we hear and all we see,
Doubt, chance, and mutability.

(11. 25-31)

In contrast to the "vain endeavour" of past sages and poets, which recalls the vain quest of the hero of *Alastor,* stands Shelley's concept of Beauty:

Thy light alone, like mist o'er mountains driven,
Or music by the night wind sent
Thro' strings of some still instrument,
Or moonlight on a midnight stream,
Gives grace and truth to life's unquiet dream.

(11. 32-36)

Shelley cannot possibly mean that his concept embodies a truer version of ultimate reality than that of former sages and poets: such an attitude would be so presumptuous and ego-tistical as to be ridiculous. He means only that his concept involves no "vain endeavour" because it postulates nothing regarding ultimate reality. In the next stanza he analyzes Beauty into "Love, Hope, and Self-esteem"—that is, into three precious feelings or states of mind—which "like clouds depart / And come, for some uncertain moments lent" (11. 37-38). Regarding the ultimate cause or metaphysical basis of these feelings or states of mind, the poet remains essentially noncommittal, describing it as "unknown":

Man were immortal and omnipotent,
Didst thou, unknown and awful as thou art,
Keep with thy glorious train firm state within his heart.

(11. 39-41)

In short, man knows nothing of Beauty as a metaphysical concept; he knows it only as a rare "state within his heart"; and only this "state within his heart" can give "grace and truth to life's unquiet dream."[21]

The concept of Beauty implied in *Alastor* and described in the *Hymn to Intellectual Beauty*—a concept not of an objective entity but of a feeling arising from an unknown cause or power—appears in other of Shelley's works. It occurs, for instance, in *Speculations on Metaphysics* (1815?): "The caverns of the mind are obscure and shadowy; or prevaded with a lustre, beautifully bright indeed, but shining not beyond their portals" (VII, 64); and in *Julian and Maddalo* (1818):

Where is the love, beauty and truth we seek,
But in our mind?

(11. 174-175)

This is a doctrine not of a solipsist but of a sceptic—a sceptic who knows only his own impressions but is far from identifying those impressions with ultimate reality.

While Shelley, however, generally conceives of Beauty as a feeling arising from an unknown cause or power, he sometimes—particularly after 1818—expresses some sceptical form of faith in its objective and independent existence. Clearly referring to an aspect of ultimate reality rather than to a state of mind, the concept embodied in these lines of *Prometheus Unbound* (1819), for instance, owes its sceptical quality primarily to its conditional form of expression:

> *How glorious art thou, Earth! And if thou be*
> *The shadow of some spirit lovelier still,*
> *Though evil stain its work, and it should be*
> *Like its creation, weak yet beautiful,*
> *I could fall down and worship that and thee.*
>
> (II. iii. 12-16)

On the other hand the concept of an absolute Beauty in the conclusion of *The Sensitive Plant* (1820) possesses a sceptical quality, not because of any conditional form of expression, but because of its admitted elusiveness: the failure of our "organs," whose vision is "obscure," to apprehend an absolute Beauty, the poet implies, constitutes no demonstration of its non-existence:

> *For love, and beauty, and delight,*
> *There is no death nor change; their might*
> *Exceeds our organs, which endure*
> *No light, being themselves obscure.*

Shelley's belief in the existence of an absolute Beauty, although it cannot be apprehended in our mortal state, reaches a climax in *Adonais* (1812) :

> *The One remains, the many change and pass;*
> *Heaven's light forever shines, Earth's shadows fly;*
> *Life, like a dome of many-coloured glass,*
> *Stains the white radiance of eternity,*
> *Until Death tramples it to fragments.—Die,*
> *If thou wouldst be with that which thou dost seek!*
>
> (11. 460-465; cf. *Hellas,* 11. 766-769)

In each case it may be said that Shelley's concept of an absolute Beauty rests on faith, not on reason.

The differences in their theories of knowledge, therefore, inevitably conducted Plato and Shelley to fundamental differences in their concepts of Beauty. Plato's concept, adapted to the doctrine of reminiscence, involves a dialectical ascent into ultimate being; whereas Shelley's, adapted to scepticism, refers only to a rare experience or to a faith in the existence of a metaphysical basis for that experience which we cannot apprehend in our mortal state. Their attitudes toward their respective concepts, as we shall now see, likewise reveal differences traceable to differences in their theories of knowledge: both men reflect something less than entire satisfaction with their doctrines of Beauty, but they do so for different reasons.

After converting the Ideas into ultimate entities discoverable by reason, Plato was soon faced by some dialectical difficulties from which he was unable to escape. Parmenides, for instance, puts the following question to Plato's Socrates, as the latter admits having expressed some things of which he is not altogether confident: "And would you feel equally undecided, Socrates, about things of which the mention may provoke a smile?—I mean such things as hair, mud, dirt, or anything else which is vile and paltry; would you suppose that each of these has an idea distinct from the actual objects with which we come into contact, or not?" Socrates grants both the pertinence of this question and the absurdity of supposing the existence of any form of Ideal Ugliness; and these admissions lead him to wonder whether the Ideas may not "be thoughts only," having "no proper existence except in our minds," in which case the Ideas "would no longer be absolute" (*Parmenides* 130-133).

Shelley likewise was not entirely satisfied with his doctrine of absolute Beauty, although the difficulties confronting him were not dialectical. They arose, instead, from deferring the possibility of apprehending absolute Beauty until after death.

By the pursuit of death, as we have already noted, Plato referred to the cultivation of an austere and disinterested dialectical pursuit of ultimate truth. But in adapting Plato's meaning to his own scepticism, Shelley substituted an attitude of otherworldliness for Plato's dialectics. Such an alternative, however, required a firm belief in the soul's immortality, whereas the poet's was most tenuous. In his notes to *Hellas,* for instance, he asserts that man's only valid basis for believing in immortality is his "inextinguishable thirst" for it: "Until better arguments can be produced than sophisms which disgrace the cause, this desire itself must remain the strongest and only presumption that eternity is the inheritance of every thinking being." That this "only presumption" was quite inadequate to banishing doubt finds expression in a sonnet of 1820 (IV, 64):

> *Ye hasten to the dead! What seek ye there,*
> *Ye restless thoughts and busy purposes*
> *Of the idle brain, which the world's livery wear?*
> *O thou quick Heart, which pantest to possess*
> *All that pale Expectation feigneth fair!*
> *Thou vainly curious Mind which wouldest guess*
> *Whence thou didst come, and whither thou must go,*
> *And that which never yet was known wouldst know—*
> *Oh, whither hasten ye, that thus ye press*
> *With such swift feet life's green and pleasant path,*
> *Seeking alike from happiness and woe*
> *A refuge in the cavern of grey death?*
> *O heart, and mind, and thoughts! what thing do you*
> *Hope to inherit in the grave below?*

It is no cause for wonder, therefore, to find Shelley sometimes exhibiting a tendency diametrically opposed to the otherworldliness of *Adonais,* that is, a tendency to identify his subjective vision of Beauty with a mortal creature. The glorification of Emilia Viviani in *Epipsychidion,* written a few months before *Adonais,* illustrates this tendency:

> *I knew it was the Vision veiled from me*
> *So many years—that it was Emily.*
>
> (11. 343-344)

Critics have often compared Shelley's *Epipsychidion* with Dante's *Vita Nuova,* but perhaps Keats' *Endymion* represents a truer parallel:

> *My sweetest Indian, here*
> *Here will I kneel, for thou redeemed hast*
> *My life from too thin breathing: Gone and past*
> *Are cloudy phantoms. Caverns lone, farewell!*
> *And air of visions, and the monstrous swell*
> *Of visionary seas! No, never more*
> *Shall airy voices cheat me to the shore*
> *Of tangled wonder, breathless and aghast.*[22]

Shelley, of course, was more at home in a rarefied atmosphere than was Keats; what he was seeking escape from in *Epipsychidion*—perhaps without being fully aware of it— was the concentration of hope upon an afterlife about which he knew that he knew nothing.[23]

In *The Triumph of Life,* left unfinished when he died in 1822, Shelley approached his problem—that of arriving at a satisfactory reconciliation of his empiricism and his idealism—from a new angle. Avoiding personal involvement by the device of assuming a spectator's point of view, he solved his problem dramatically. This fact, I think, accounts for the unusually subdued tone of the poem. Shelley transfers his faith in an absolute Beauty to the "sacred few"—

> *who could not tame*
> *Their spirits to the conquerors—but as soon*
> *As they had touched the world with living flame,*
> *Fled back like eagles to their native noon...*
>
> (11. 128-131)

But the poet is to be identified with the "sacred few" no more than with Rousseau, whose courage failed before their vision,[24] so that he followed the "cold bright car" of worldly life. How Shelley might have ended his last great poem can only be conjectured, but it is difficult to see how he could have abandoned the dramatic point of view that governs much of the work as it stands.

Shelley, then, is not a pseudo-Platonist but a Platonist in the sceptical tradition. The renascence of Platonism in his mature writings—a development that previous critics have never satisfactorily explained—owed much to the poet's investigation of the sceptical tradition during the years 1813-1816. Scepticism liberated Shelley from the prejudice against Platonism which he had inherited from the French materialists and rationalists of the eighteenth century: it accomplished this result by depicting Plato as a poet of the unknown and unknowable and as a forerunner of the sceptical point of view in philosophy. But scepticism not only formed a transition between Shelley's early materialism and his later Platonism but also determined the specific character of that later Platonism. When they came to adapt the concept of Beauty to their respective theories of knowledge, Plato and Shelley faced different tasks, which led to different results. His theory of reminiscence enabled Plato to seek Beauty dialectically as an aspect of ultimate reality. On the other hand, Shelley's sceptical theory of knowledge led him to conceive of Beauty as the unknown cause of a fleeting sense of ecstasy, or as an aspect of reality supported only by faith.

VI

SCEPTICISM AND CHRISTIANITY

IT is difficult to conceive a subject that offers greater obstacles to objective treatment than the religion of a poet whom one either admires or dislikes, for one's feeling toward the poet as well as one's own religious views tend to color the discussion. There can be no doubt of Shelley's familiarity with and extensive use of the Bible[1], nor of his veneration for Jesus.[2] But how far the poet's religious views conform to Christianity is another question. According to some critics, Shelley was irreconcilably opposed to Christianity,[3] according to others, he deviated from his ancestral faith only in particular respects—in portraying evil as "purely external to man"[4] or the Supreme Being as "altogether benevolent."[5] Our purpose here, however, is not to define the degree to which Shelley conformed to Christian doctrine, but to investigate the influence of scepticism—a term that we cantinue to use in its classic sense—on his attitude toward organized Christianity.

This subject has received little attention. Recently, however, Frederick L. Jones suggested that Shelley's growing awareness of the limitations of reason almost reconciled him with the Christian religion; then, rereading Wordsworth's poems in 1815, the poet discovered "a way towards religion which greatly appealed to him because it made it possible for him to escape both Atheism and Christianity."[6] The present chapter will examine this provocative theory as well as the possibility of fideism in the apparently conventional use of the word God in Shelley's later poems.

At the beginning of 1811, when Shelley and Hogg composed *The Necessity of Atheism,* the poet's knowledge of the sceptical tradition was both superficial and fragmentary, derived largely from some of Hume's *Essays.* While Hume's *Essays,* therefore, was one of the sources used by Shelley and Hogg, their tract, far from conforming to the spirit of scepticism, is remarkably rigid and dogmatic. Belief, according to the youthful authors, is an involuntary passion traceable to "three degrees of excitement": the evidence of the senses, reason, and testimony. The strongest degree of excitement comes from the evidence of the senses, and the next strongest from reason ultimately based on the evidence of the senses. Testimony not only provides the lowest degree of excitement but is quite without any validity when opposed to reason. Since none of the proofs known to them regarding the existence of God survives this analysis of the sources of conviction, Shelley and Hogg conclude: "Every reflecting mind must allow that there is no proof of the existence of a Deity" (V, 207-209).

Although Shelley continued to reject the idea of a creative God, he did not long remain an advocate of atheism. Nor, as we noted in an earlier chapter, did he long remain unaware of the limitations of reason and of the role of the feelings in the shaping of beliefs (see above, pp. 46-48). In a letter dated June 2, 1812, for instance, he wrote to Elizabeth Hitchener: "I have much to talk to you of. Innate Passions, God, Christianity, etc., when we meet. Would not 'co-existent with our organization' be a more correct phrase for passions than 'innate'? I think I can prove to you that *our* God is the same." Thus a growing awareness of the limitations of reason and the discovery of Hume's theory of innate passions led Shelley tacitly to renounce certain aspects of *The Necessity of Atheism.* The revised version of this tract which was included in the Notes to *Queen Mab,* in the poet's own words, "must be understood solely to affect a creative Deity. The hypothesis of a pervading Spirit coeternal with the universe, remains unshaken" (I, 146).

A comparison of *The Necessity of Atheism* with *A Refutation of Deism* (1814) discloses more important evidence of the influence of scepticism on Shelley's religious thought. While *The Necessity of Atheism* belongs to a materialist variety of dogmatism, *A Refutation of Deism* conforms in every respect to the sceptical tradition. Insufficiently aware of this basic difference, previous critics have misinterpreted the motive of the later pamphlet. The traditional interpretation, as expressed by Newman I. White,[7] is that in writing *A Refutation of Deism* Shelley was indulging in irony, which afforded him the pleasure both of abusing Christianity and of escaping prosecution. Frederick L. Jones, on the other hand, interprets the pamphlet literally and arrives at an exactly opposite conclusion: "As a step in Shelley's development, the pamphlet can mean nothing else than that Shelley, dissatisfied with the inevitable *Atheism* to which his materialistic philosophy led, had tried Deism and had found it as fatally deficient, and had concluded that there was no true religion except a religion based on revelation, of which type Christianity was the highest."[8] Neither of these two interpretations, it appears to me, is entirely acceptable.

A Refutation of Deism is a dialogue on theology. The dialogue begins with Eusebes' defence of Christianity, followed by Theosophus' attack on it. Eusebes then challenges Theosophus to state his grounds of belief in God, so that Eusebes might point out their weakness, thus demonstrating that the only alternative to atheism is faith in Christianity. Theosophus presents his grounds of belief in God and Eusebes points out their defects. The dialogue ends with Theosophus' admission that he is unprepared to answer his adversary's "unexpected arguments"; should those arguments prove incontrovertible after mature deliberation, he promises "to adopt so much of the Christian scheme as is consistent with my persuasion of the goodness, unity and majesty of God" (VI, 27-57). While Shelley borrowed material, as the notes indicate, from a variety of sources, his pamphlet belongs to the same genre as Cicero's *De natura deorum,* Hume's *Dialogues Concerning Natural Religion,* and the dialogue in Chapter IV of Drummond's *Academical Questions.* Each of these works is a dialogue on theology written by an avowed sceptic and containing at least one spokesman for scepticism, whose views need not in every respect represent those of the author.

The spokesman for scepticism in Shelley's pamphlet is Eusebes, who in the very first paragraph refers to the narrow limits of the human understanding: "To this excess then has the pride of the human understanding at length arrived? To measure itself with Omniscience! To scan the intentions of Inscrutability!" Pointing to the failure of the theists of antiquity to establish belief in "one Almighty God" on rational grounds (VI, 30), he concludes that "faith is superior to reason, in as much as the creature is surpassed by the Creator;

and that whensoever they are incompatible, the suggestions of the latter, not those of the former, are to be questioned" (VI, 31). Underlying Eusebes' scepticism is his acceptance of Hume's theory of cause: "Hume has shewn, to the satisfaction of all philosophers, that the only idea which we can form of causation is derivable from the constant conjunction of objects, and the consequent inference of one from the other" (VI, 55).

Some of Eusebes' arguments, to be sure, are derived from materialist sources. But such arguments, unlike Hume's theory of cause, do not represent a part of his own thought, though they indirectly support it. Eusebes borrows material, for instance, from Holbach's *Le Système de la Nature,* described in a note as "one of the most eloquent vindications of Atheism" (VI, 54). In their context, however, Eusebes' arguments drawn from materialist sources serve only to illustrate the inadequacy of reason in matters pertaining to religion. According to one such argument, each of God's attributes is either borrowed from the passions and powers of the human mind or constitutes a negation; according to another, we know intelligence only "as a mode of animal being": the deist's Supreme Intelligence, therefore, must be "a vast and wise animal" (VI, 54-55). The function of such arguments is to convert the underlying assumption of natural theology—that a religion can be erected on a rational foundation—into a *reductio ad absurdum.* Such materialist arguments support scepticism but are not an integral part of it.

If our classification of *A Refutation of Deism* is sound, we must reject its traditional interpretation. The dialogue is ironical in a philosophical rather than in a satirical manner; it is ironical in the maner of Cicero's *De natura deorum,* not in the manner of Swift's *A Modest Proposal.* All scepticism is in one sense of the word ironical, for it employs reason to demonstrate the limitations of reason. But such irony is never deliberate, never the mere expression of the author's will; it is an inescapable result of his mode of reasoning.

On the other hand, the theory that Shelley was about to embrace Christianity on a fideistic basis, in the manner advocated by Eusebes, is also untenable. It is true that sceptics, despairing of ever settling any ultimate question through reason, have often advocated the acceptance of a traditional religion on faith. But there are many exceptions to this rule, and Shelley's principal models—Cicero, Hume, Drummond—were all exceptions. At the conclusion of the *De natura deorum* Cicero expresses a preference for the theology of Stoicism over the ancestral creed defended by his fellow-sceptic. In the *Dialogues Concerning Natural Religion* Philo, who probably speaks for Hume, concludes with a surprising note of friendliness toward the deism which he had just refuted; while Drummond's religious speculations are less fideistic than deistic. Shelley, in fact, considered both Hume and Drummond deists (X, 112); and so they are to the extent that scepticism and deism are reconcilable through the doctrine of probability.

Furthermore, Shelley's hostility toward Christianity was primarily based not on metaphysical but moral grounds, upon which his acquistion of a sceptical point of view was not necessarily bound to exercise any influence. Moral objections to popular religions may be found in Hume's writings—particularly in his *Natural History of Religion*. But such objections are neither confined to the works of sceptics nor bear any necessary relation to them. Moral objections to popular religion occur in the writings of a number of rationalists referred to in the notes to *A Refutation of Deism*. Spinoza, for instance, defined popular religion "as respect for ecclesiastics. The spread of this misconception inflamed every worthless fellow with an intense desire to enter holy orders, and thus the love of diffusing God's religion degenerated into sordid avarice and ambition."[9] And according to Thomas Paine's *Age of Reason*: "All national institutions of churches, whether Jewish, Christian or Turkish, appear to be no other than human inventions, set up to terrify and enslave mankind, and monopolize power and profit."[10]

The poet's moral objections to Christianity, however, arose not only from his reading but also from the reactionary status of organized Christianity in his own time and place. Frightened by the French Revolution, the clergy had become distrustful of all reform proposals. "Shelley, the atheist," remarks Sister Anna Mercedes, "blasted *nineteenth century* Christianity. Had Augustine been alive he would have helped him."[11] And Hoxie Neale Fairchild declares that at a time when organized Christianity "was even more than usually reactionary in matters political, social, and intellectual, it needed to be stung by such a gadfly" as Shelley.[12] In short, the moral objections to Christianity which Shelley met with in Thomas Paine and other writers appeared to be confirmed by his own observations of society.

While the young poet, accordingly, employed metaphysical arguments in dealing with the question of the existence of God, in dealing with Christianity he tended to confine his attack to moral objections. So he himself pointed out in an undated letter to Janetta Philipps written in 1811: "As you mention Religion, I will say, that my rejection of *revealed* proceeds from my perfect conviction of its insufficiency to the happiness of man—to this source I can trace murder, war, intolerance—my rejection of *natural* arises wholly from *reason*. I *once* was an enthusiastic Deist, but never a Christian." Murder, war, and intolerance would suit the taste of the Christian God described in *Queen Mab*—the God:

Who, prototype of human misrule, sits
High in heaven's realm, upon a golden throne ...

(VI, 105-106)

Most of Shelley's philosophical arguments against natural religion applied, of course, to Christianity as well; but his attacks on Christianity largely ignored this fact to concentrate on apparent weaknesses more serious than those of defective logic.

The same tendency appears in *A Refutation*, for Theosophus' attack on Christianity, unlike Eusebes' attack on deism, is based largely on moral grounds. Where, asks Theosophus, can one find "a record of such grovelling absurdities and enormities so atrocious, a picture of the Deity so characteristic of a demon as that which the sacred writings of the Jews contain"? He refers to the God who "expressly commanded Moses to invade an unoffending nation, and on account of the difference of their worship utterly to destroy every human being it contained, to murder every infant and unarmed man in cold blood, to massacre the captives, to rip up the matrons, and to retain the maidens alone for concubinage and violation" (VI, 34). Gibbon as well as the Bible furnishes Theosophus with examples of the immorality of Christianity. Regarding Constantine's punishment of unlicenced love, Theosophus remarks: "This cold-blooded and hypocritical ruffian cut his son's throat, strangled his wife, murdered his father-in-law and his brother-in-law, and maintained at his court a set of blood-thirsty and bigoted Christian priests, one of whom was sufficient to excite the one half of the world to massacre the other" (VI, 38). Only when he attacks belief in miracles and prophecies (VI, 39-42) do Theosophus' objections to Christianity assume an abstract and distinterested character.

A Refutation of Deism is by virtue of its genre ambiguous

and inconclusive. It ends with the promise of Theosophus "to adopt so much of the Christian scheme as is consistent with my persuasion of the goodness, unity and majesty of God" (VI, 57). This cryptic remark, in so far as it expresses Shelley's own sentiments, can be adequately understood only in the light of the *Essay on Christianity*, which was probably written in 1816.[13] Shelley was willing to embrace on faith only so much of the "Christian scheme" as was free from the moral objections noted above. In essence this qualification meant that he drew a sharp distinction between historic Christianity and Jesus Christ, interpreting the teachings of the latter as those of a kind of idealistic sceptic.

Certain obstacles, Shelley admits, confront one who desires a precise ascertainment of Christ's teachings. Since the founder of Christianity has left no written record of himself, one must depend upon "the imperfect and obscure information which his biographers, persons certainly of very undisciplined and undiscriminating minds, have transmitted to posterity." The records of these "biographers" are unreliable because they contain fundamental contradictions, presenting "in the midst of a strain of impassioned eloquence, or sagest exhortation, a sentiment only remarkable for its naked and drivelling folly." A sentiment of this kind, according to Shelley, cannot be ascribed to Christ; it is an invention of one of Christ's "undisciplined and undiscriminating" biographers. The real Christ consistently combined simplicity and nobility; he was "a man of meek and majestic demeanor, calm in danger, of natural and simple thoughts and habits, beloved to adoration by his adherents, unmoved and solemn and serene" (VI, 240-241).

One aspect of traditional Christianity which Shelley regarded as morally objectionable was the belief that "the body shall live after its apparent dissolution, and be rendered capable of indefinite torture." Christ viewed this "absurd and execrable doctrine of vengeance," according to Shelley, "with the profoundest disapprobation." Belief in hell, the poet implies, is one of the inventions of Christ's biographers which flatly contradicts other assertions ascribed to Christ: that we should love our enemies if we would be the sons of our Heavenly Father; that God makes the sun to shine on the good and on the evil, and the rain to fall on the just and the unjust (VI, 232-233).

Shelley's views on the belief in heaven are more complex than his views on the belief in hell. He rejects the idea of heaven as an eternal reward for good behavior on earth, but looks with indulgence upon the doctrine of immortal bliss as an expression of the poetic imagination. The former conception of heaven, according to Shelley, is foreign to the teachings of Christ, "who has said no more than the most excellent philosophers have felt and expressed—that virtue is its own reward" (VI, 230). All that Christ taught on the subject of heaven is that death will bring individual happiness to all men and an end to all evil and pain—a magnificent conception "even if no more than the imagination of some sublimest and most holy poet, who impressed with the loveliness and majesty of his own nature, is impatient and discontented, with the narrow limits which this imperfect life and dark grave have assigned for ever as his melancholy portion" (VI, 236).

Perhaps nothing alienated Shelley so much from traditional Christianity as his conception of its reactionary bias— to which he opposed his conception of Christ as a political radical. Christ, according to Shelley, believed in the equality of men. Like Plato and Diogenes, the founder of Christianity recognized that in the absence of such equality men cultivate their "meaner wants to so great an excess as to judge nothing valuable or desirable but what relates to their gratification."

This process, in turn, gives rise to "a system of passions which loses sight of the end which they were originally to attain" (VI, 244-247). Christ's doctrine of the equality of men, however, was destroyed by "demagogues of the infant republic of the Christian sect." These "demagogues" silenced the moral sense among men by engaging them "to attend not so much to the cultivation of a virtuous and happy life in this mortal scene as to the attainment of a fortunate condition after death; not so much to the consideration of those means by which the state of man is adorned and improved as an enquiry into the secrets of the connection between God and the world, things which they well knew were not to be explained or even to be conceived" (VI, 251).

That Shelley regarded Christ's theological doctrines as consistent with scepticism has already been suggested in our review of the poet's comments on Christ's ideas on hell, heaven, and the equality of men. But the conception of God which Shelley ascribes to Christ is even more remarkable for its sceptical quality. While the name of God, according to the poet, had been "profanely perverted to the sanctioning of the most enormous and abominable crimes," Christ held that God is "some universal being, differing from man and from the mind of man." "It is important," Shelley continues, "to observe that the author of the Christian system had a conception widely differing from the gross imaginations of the vulgar relatively to the ruling Power of the universe. He everywhere represents this power as something mysteriously and illimitably pervading the frame of things." Nor did Christ ever contradict himself on this subject by representing this "limitless and inconceivable mystery" as a being subject to passion (VI, 229-230).

If Shelley regarded Christ as a kind of sceptic, he was able to do so, in the first place, because he completely rejected the doctrine of Christ's divinity. The founder of Christianity, according to the poet, belongs to a class of illustrious mortals who were devoted to their fellowmen; what distinguishes Christ from the other "martyrs and patriots" is "the profound wisdom and the comprehensive morality of his doctrines" (VI, 227). Some years later— in *A Defence of Poetry* (III, 124) and the Prologue to *Hellas* (11. 94-95) —Shelley was to suggest that Christ was a disciple of Plato, whom sceptics traditionally regarded as one of their precursors.

Shelley's attitude toward Christianity changed after his composition of the *Essay on Christianity* only in such respects as those noted by Mr. Stovall. *The Cenci* and portions of *Hellas* are evidence that the mature poet learned to treat opinions of Christian characters objectively, in accordance with the requirements of dramatic art. Furthermore, a passage in *A Defence of Poetry* (III, 123) indicates that Shelley came to recognize a connection between the spread of Christianity and the rise of certain reforms, namely, the abolition of slavery and the emancipation of women.[14]

But these concessions to dramatic art and to historical fact did not lead Shelley to retract his moral objections to Christianity. In fact, the main theme of the *Essay on Christianity*— the distinction between Christ's teachings and the Christian religion—occurs in passages of Shelley's mature works. In *Prometheus Unbound,* for instance, Shelley represents Christ's spirit as tormented by the distortion of his message among Christians:

> *Hark that outcry of despair!*
> *'Tis the mild and gentle ghost*
> *Wailing for the faith he kindled. . . .*
> (I, 533-556)

The central idea of the *Essay on Christianity* occurs also in the Prologue to *Hellas*, though cast in the words of a jeering Satan:

> *Art thou eyeless like old Destiny,*
> *Thou mockery-king, crowned with a wreath of thorns?*
> *Whose sceptre is a reed, the broken reed*
> *Which pierces thee! whose throne a chair of scorn;*
> *For seest thou not beneath this crystal floor*
> *The innumerable worlds of golden light*
> *Which are my empire. . . .*
>
> (ll. 121-127)

Finally, a passage in *The Triumph of Life* recalls the "demagogues of the infant republic of the Christian sect" who, according to the *Essay on Christianity*, early succeeded in corrupting Christ's teachings for posterity:

> *And Gregory and John, and men divine,*
>
> *Who rose like shadows between men and God;*
> *Till that eclipse, still hanging over heaven,*
> *Was worshipped by the world o'er which they strode,*
>
> *For the true sun it quenched . . .*
>
> (ll. 88-92)

But while Shelley hardly changed his attitude toward Christianity after he wrote the *Essay on Christianity*, in the last few years of his life he not infrequently employed the name of God in his poetry in what appears to be an orthodox and conventional manner. One of the earliest examples of this tendency occurs in *The Masque of Anarchy* (1819):

> *Let a vast assembly be,*
> *And with great solemnity*
> *Declare with measured words that ye*
> *Are, as God has made ye, free. . . .*
>
> (11. 299-302)

Another example is the often quoted passage from *The Boat on the Serchio* (1821):

> *All rose to do the task He set to each,*
> *Who shaped us to His ends and not our own. . . .*
>
> (11. 30-31)

In *The Triumph of Life* (1822) Shelley wonders

> *why God made irreconcilable*
> *Good and the means of good . . .*
>
> (11. 230-231)

Other examples may be found in *The Sensitive Plant* (11. 115-118), the *Ode to Naples* (11. 69-71), the *Sonnet to Byron* (11. 7-8), and *Adonais* (11. 166-167). In all these examples, so far as one can ascertain, the words are spoken by the poet himself, not by a distinguishable narrator or other dramatic character. The passages, therefore, cannot be explained as the result of the requirements of dramatic art.

These passages have elicited various inferences from Shelley's critics. Robert Browning surmised that "had Shelley lived he would have finally ranged himself with the Christians."[15] According to Newman I. White, on the other hand, "there are occasions on which he [Shelley] uses the word God in the conventional way in which it was used around him by regular Christians, but these are palpable slips."[16] Ellsworth Barnard, however, feels that "it is the critic who is here guilty of a 'palpable slip.' Aside from the frequency of these 'slips,' it is significant that they are confined entirely to the later poems."[17] Mr. Barnard's conclusion is that Shelley finally came to believe in the existence of a personal God.

Though apparently supported by the passages referred to above, this conclusion contradicts the poet's frequent assertion that God is an inconceivable power differing from man and the mind of man. Furthermore, belief in the existence of a personal God would have gone far toward invalidating Shelley's distinction between Christ's doctrines and Christianity; but, as we have noted, this distinction appears intact in Shelley's mature works. On the other hand, it is true that the occasions on which Shelley uses the name of God in an apparently orthodox and conventional manner are too frequent to be dismissed as "slips." One wonders, therefore, whether the use of the word God in Shelley's later poems may not be less orthodox and conventional than at first appears.

It may be inferred from the *Essay on Christianity* that Shelley employed the name of God in two quite different senses, neither of which may be described as conventional. He used the word God to mean either the cruel "demon" allegedly worshipped by Christians or the inconceivable and impersonal power allegedly worshipped by Christ. The God in Shelley's mature poems is probably identical with the latter use of the term—like "the unknown God" twice mentioned in *Hellas* (11. 211, 735). What appears, therefore, to be a contradiction in his conception of the governing principle of the universe may result entirely from an erroneous assumption—the assumption that the word God in his later poems is employed in a conventional sense.

Even in his youth Shelley occasionally used the word God in a favorable but unconventional sense, as, for instance, when he wrote to Elizabeth Hitchener concerning *"our* God," defined as a passion "co-existent with our organization." But the young poet did not employ the word God, except in discussing Christ's doctrines in the *Essay on Christianity,* to signify an inconceivable and illimitable power governing the universe. Why he came to do so in his later poems can only be conjectured. Perhaps he was influenced by the references to God in Dante, Calderón, and other great Christian poets. But that his concept was not identical with theirs is evident from his letter to Horace Smith, dated April 11, 1822, wherein he remarks that the doctrines of materialism, though "false as they are pernicious," are "still better than Christianity."

Scepticism, therefore, had little influence on Shelley's attitude toward Christianity, which remained consistently hostile to the end of his life. But scepticism influenced his religious thought in a number of other ways. It led the poet to conclude that faith and not reason must constitute the main support of any religion. It led him to reject the dogmatic method of *The Necessity of Atheism* and to adopt the artfully ambiguous and inconclusive method of *A Refutation of Deism.* It colored his interpretation of Christ's teachings— especially his interpretation of Christ's idea of God. But at no time did scepticism come near to converting Shelley to Christianity, for his hostility to it consistently rested on moral and not metaphysical arguments. The theory, therefore, that Wordsworth played an important part in the evolution of Shelley's religious thought appears erroneous: first, because Shelley was not about to embrace Christianity in 1815; and, secondly, because he had discovered an escape from both atheism and Christianity long before 1815 and independently of Wordsworth. In his later poems Shelley often uses the name of God in what appears to be a conventional sense; in all probability, however, the name refers to the unconventional idea of God described in the *Essay on Christianity*—a mysterious being, differing from man and the mind of man.

VII

DURING the years 1811-1816 much of Shelley's reading in philosophy was devoted to sceptics. Hume and Drummond familiarized him with the most recent developments in sceptical thought — developments interpreted by Hume's chief British adversaries, the Common Sense school of thinkers, as the logical and inevitable result of a doctrine pervading nearly all modern speculation. Cicero and Diogenes Laertius introduced Shelley to the scepticism of antiquity; Sir Thomas Browne and Montaigne, to the scepticism of the Renaissance. The impact on the poet's mind of the sceptical tradition, as variously represented by these authors, is largely responsible for those modifications in his thought which critics have long recognized as distinguishing the mature from the young Shelley.

To appreciate, however, the possibility of this conclusion, it is necessary to bear in mind that the sceptical tradition, from its origin down to Shelley's own time, possesses a positive side as well as a negative, and that the former rests on disparate principles. On its negative side scepticism attempts to demonstrate the limitations of reason and knowledge. Sceptics differ on this point only in degree, that is, in the thoroughness and depth of their arguments. But on its positive side scepticism branches off into dissimilar principles; sceptics disagree in their sceptical solutions to doubt. Some rely mainly on custom, others on faith, still others on the doctrine of probability. The main difference lies between the first and the last of these solutions, while the second is compatible with either of the other two. The reliance on custom naturally leads to the adoption of conservative ideas. Probabilism, on the other hand, may and often does conduct to unorthodox views.

The fundamental doctrine on the negative side of Shelley's scepticism is a theory of causation—a theory that the poet first encountered in Godwin; its full implications, however, did not dawn on him until after he read and reread Hume and Drummond. All knowledge, according to this theory, depends on the relationship which we call cause and effect. But a scrupulous examination of this relationship reveals that the concept is founded on habit, that it arises from our experience of the constant conjunction of objects. Such an analysis of cause and effect banishes at once all possibility of certitude on any matter whatsoever. A provisional science, based on the observation of the constant conjunction of objects, is altogether possible. But where the opportunity of observing the constant conjunction of objects is denied us—which is the case in cosmological, ontological, and theological speculations —reasoning from cause to effect collapses into an exercise of the fancy. Thus reason conducts us to an astonishing awareness of our ignorance; in Shelley's words, we reach "the verge where words abandon us, and what wonder if we grow dizzy to look down the dark abyss of how little we know" (VI, 196).

But like every sceptic before him, Shelley cultivated a

sceptical solution to doubt, even to the extent of expressing various degrees of assent to propositions regarding ultimate reality. He nowhere relies on custom to escape the sceptic's dilemma, as conformity to the *status quo* was quite incompatible with his social philosophy, his passion for reforming the world. But either faith or the doctrine of probability is implicit in all of his affirmations regarding the transcendent. By overlooking their tentative character or conditional nature, we may confound these with otherwise similar affirmations in Coleridge or Wordsworth or Emerson; Shelley's affirmations, however, are not dogmatic intuitions but aspects of his sceptical solution to doubt. And it is their character as such that gives them their distinctive quality and effect.

The charges of inconsistency not infrequently made against Shelley's thought, especially by recent scholars, are the direct result of the overlooking of this distinction. These charges appear baseless when the poet's thought is interperted, as it should be interpreted, partly in the light of the sceptical tradition. It is true, of course, that Holbach's necessarianism and Berkeley's idealism can hardly be integrated into a coherent metaphysics. That Shelley's thought sometimes reflects such irreconcilable elements rests on two assumptions: that the poet rejected common-sense materialism through Berkeley's influence and that his concept of Necessity agrees with that of the French materialists. Both of these assumptions, however, are erroneous.

There is not the slightest evidence that Berkeley had any significant influence on Shelley's rejection of common-sense materialism. In fact, the poet plainly tells us that Berkeley's arguments did not impress him. What led Shelley to reject common-sense materialism was Hume's theory of causation as applied by both Hume and Drummond to the question of the independent existence of external objects: we cannot assume the existence of a material world as the cause of our sensations, for all we know of cause is the constant conjunction of ideas in our own mind; the cause of our sensations is unknown.

It is true, of course, that Shelley makes affirmations regarding this unknown reality; but these have the sceptical character of resting on faith or probability. Furthermore, his clearest positive remark about ultimate reality is that it must differ from mind; for it is supremely creative, while mind is largely passive. Nothing could be further from Berkeley than this doctrine. On the other hand, Shelley's theory of the "one mind," of which all individual minds are a portion, resembles Berkeley; but the resemblance is quite superficial: Shelley's concept refers to something less than "the basis of all things" or reality; hence, it is quite unlike Berkeley's idea of an infinite mind acting as the cause of phenomena.

Just as Shelley's scepticism renders his idealism significantly unlike Berkeley's, so it makes his doctrine of Necessity significantly unlike that of the French materialists. Shelley's doctrine is not dogmatic, nor does it subsume a materialist world-view. Its source was Hume's theory of causation and the restatement of that theory in Godwin and Drummond. As an historical concept, Shelley's Necessity refers to the constant conjunction of events observable in the evolution of society.[1] As a metaphysical concept, which is the main concern here, it is the unknown cause of our sensations, the mysterious principle that governs the universe. The poet's interpretation of this unknown power as favoring the triumph of good over evil is partly the expression of faith, partly a form of probabilism based on the study of historical evolution.

Due attention to Shelley's scepticism disposes not only of the alleged inconsistency between his idealism and necessarianism, but also of his alleged pseudo-Platonism. By liberating him from the prejudices against the Greek philosopher which he had inherited from the *philosophes,* scepticism was to an important degree responsible for the renascence of Platonism which occurred in Shelley in 1817. But it was responsible also for the poet's considerable deviation from Plato. Shelley's concept of Beauty, unlike Plato's, is not dialectically arrived at; nor does it involve a theory of ultimate reality— except the sceptic's denial of the possibility of man's knowing ultimate reality. It is essentially an "unknown and awful" power, which man apprehends only as an ecstasy "within his heart" (*Hymn to Intellectual Beauty*). Sometimes Shelley expresses the faith that death will reveal to us this "unknown and awful power" in all its splendor (*Adonais*), but this tendency of thought is counterbalanced by the opposite one of seeking Beauty in a concrete and mortal form (*Epipsychidion*). In brief, Shelley is not a pseudo-Platonist but a consistent Platonist in the sceptical tradition.

But while scepticism presented Plato to Shelley in a new light, it had little effect on his hostility toward organized Christianity. As a sceptic, the poet agreed with the fideists that the main bulwark of any religion is faith, not reason. But this admission did not imply the result one might expect: the sceptic Shelley is almost as hostile toward organized Christianity as the materialist Shelley had been. From his early reading of anti-Christian authors and from his own experience of the reactionary and intolerant character of early nineteenth-century Christianity, Shelley had come to entertain certain moral objections to the Christian religion. These would have remained obstacles to his reconciliation with his ancestral creed regardless of what metaphysical views he later embraced. He was willing, as a sceptic, to accept as much of the Christian religion as was free from his moral objections to it. But the qualification included too much of the Christian religion to allow any real departure from his original unfavorable attitude. The references to "God" in his later poems—which suggest to some critics that the poet was becoming more orthodox in his religious opinions—probably refer to the deity whom he thought Christ worshipped: a mysterious and inconceivable being, differing from man and the mind of man. Shelley's acceptance of God in this sense in no way contradicts his continued strictures against the Christian religion.

Read, then, in the light of the sceptical tradition, Shelley's philosophy reveals itself as remarkably consistent and coherent. The assertion that the poet "never lost a piece of intellectual baggage which he had at any time collected" has no foundation in fact: Shelley did not "collect" ideas in the mechanical manner implied; furthermore, he did discard ideas —like those essential to materialism—in the course of his intellectual development. Nor was Shelley "an enthusiast" who adopted any attractive idea "without first ascertaining whether it was consistent with others previously avowed." On the contrary, he resisted a new idea, as the history of his attitude toward immaterialism suggests, until the relation of that idea to others previously avowed became perfectly clear to him; or he modified ideas before adopting them, as the sceptical quality of his Platonism indicates, if in their original form they were inconsistent with his established convictions.

What bearing, one may now enquire, has this monograph upon the evaluation of Shelley as a poet?

A theoretical world-view is not essential to great poetry: the *Iliad* and *The Book of Job* both antedate the emergence of philosophy. On the other hand, any respectable theoretical system of thought is compatible with the highest poetic achievement: materialism served Lucretius as well as scholasticism served Dante.[2] Yet nothing incorporated in a poem is logically irrelevant to the evaluation of that poem. If form and content are inseparable in a given work of art, any irreconcilable philosophical elements in it, unless they serve a special purpose, must be viewed as a defect. "Between artistic coherence . . . and philosophical coherence there is some kind of correlation."[3]

If this principle of literary theory is in general sound, Shelley's scepticism is important because it provides us with a possible clue to the unity of his thought in all its variety. To begin with, scepticism is quite compatible with the four main traditions that shaped his mind—political radicalism, empiricism, Platonism, and Christianity. While scepticism is in conflict with the metaphysical views of most radicals, it is not in conflict with political radicalism as such. Scepticism and empiricism are also harmonious; in fact, all the more elaborate forms of scepticism are inseparable from empirical premises. Not unrelated, too, are scepticism and Platonism; for an idealist may make profound concessions to scepticism, while a sceptic may develop the positive side of his thought into a qualified idealism. So closely related, finally, are the sceptical and Christian traditions that the real problem here is to explain why sometimes, as in the case of Shelley, their reconciliation is incomplete.

But scepticism not only is quite compatible with the main traditions known to have profoundly influenced Shelley, but also is capable of reconciling two of those traditions that normally stand in disagreement. The central conflict in Shelley's philosophy is that between his empiricism and his Platonism. The poet's resolution of this conflict could have been suggested only by a philosopher who had dealt with the same problem: this consideration eliminates a host of philosophers known to have influenced Shelley in other respects, including Plato and Hume. The most plausible theory to date is that in this question Shelley was a disciple of Berkeley. But Shelley's relation to Hume invalidates this theory—a theory that can only lead to the conclusion that the poet was a confused follower of Berkeley. There remains, however, the possibility of reconciling empiricism and Platonism through the positive issues of scepticism—probability and faith. This mode of reconciling the empirical and Platonic traditions was implied in Drummond's *Academical Questions*. That Shelley employed the same mode is supported by his admiration for Drummond, by his relation to Hume and the sceptical tradition, and by a certain note in his idealism—a note ranging from the tentative to the mystical. In other words, scepticism had consequences in Shelley which it did not have in Hume; and it is in these consequences, not in the mere agreement with Hume, that the real significance of the poet's scepticism is to be found.

NOTES

NOTES TO CHAPTER I

1. *The Complete Works of Percy Bysshe Shelley*, Julian Edition (London, 1926-30). All references to Shelley's works, unless otherwise indicated, are to this edition.
2. *The Romantic Quest* (New York, 1931) , p. 386.
3. "Shelley's Doctrine of Love," *PMLA*, VL (1930), 283.
4. *Essays*, First Series (Boston, 1855) , pp. 50-51.
5. Johann Wolfgang Goethe, *Gedenkausgabe der Werke, Briefe und Gespräche*, herausgegeben von Ernst Beutler (Zürich, 1949), V, 9.
6. *Oeuvres Complètes de J. J. Rousseau* (Paris, 1824), XIX, 7.
7. *Sämtliche Werke* (Vienna, 1846), VIII, 100; quoted in John C. Blankenagel, "The Dominant Characteristics of German Romanticism," in "Romanticisim: A Symposium," *PMLA*, LV (1940), 7.
8. For some account of the scepticism in Keats, see Fairchild, *The Romantic Quest*, p. 419, and *Religious Trends in English Poetry* (New York, 1949), III, 474-475.

NOTES TO CHAPTER II

1. E. Zeller, *The Stoics, Epicureans, and Sceptics*, trans. Oswald J. Reichel (London, 1880) , p. 530.
2. References to Diogenes Laertius' *Lives and Opinions of Eminent Philosophers* are to the translation of R. D. Hicks in the Loeb Classical Library.

3. *Hypotyposes* i. 28. I have used the translation of the Rev. R. G. Bury in the Loeb Classical Library.

4. References to Cicero's *Academica* are to the translation of H. Rackham in the Loeb Classical Library.

5. Cf. Maurice De Wulf, *History of Medieval Philosophy*, trans. P. Coffey (London, 1909), pp. 382, 427-429.

6. *Essayes,* trans. John Florio (London, 1928) , II, 321-323.

7. *The Advancement of Learning,* ed. William Aldis Wright (Oxford, 1920), pp. 5-10.

8. *Religio Medici,* ed. Ernest Rhys, Everyman's Library (London, 1906), p. 11.

9. Louis I. Bredvold, *The Intellectual Milieu of John Dryden* (Ann Arbor, 1934), pp. 58-72.

10. *A Treatise of Human Nature* and *Dialogues Concerning Natural Religion,* ed. T. H. Green and T. H. Grosse (London, 1890), I, 311.

11. *The Works of John Locke* (London, 1794) , I, 77-79.

12. *The Works of George Berkeley,* ed. Alexander Campbell Fraser (Oxford, 1871), I, 169.

13. *Essays,* ed. T. H. Green and T. H. Grosse (London, 1889) , II, 113, 132, 359.

14. Cf. Rachael M. Kydd, *Reason and Conduct in Hume's Treatise* (London, 1946), p. 38.

15. *Essays,* II, 107, 309.

NOTES TO CHAPTER III

1. "The Life of Percy Bysshe Shelley," in Humbert Wolfe, ed., *The Life of Percy Bysshe Shelley* (London, 1933) , I, 71.

2. The exact date of this prose fragment is unknown. Internal evidence strongly supports the year 1819: see Adele B. Ballman, "The Dating of Shelley's Prose Fragments—'On Life,' 'On Love,' 'On the Punishment of Death,'" *ELH,* II (1935), 332-334; and James A. Notopoulos, "The Dating of Shelley's Prose," *PMLA,* LVIII (1942), 489 ff.

3. Preface to *Essays, Letters from Abroad, Translations, and Fragments* (London, 1840), in Shelley's *Works,* V, vii-xv.

4. "Shelley's Relation to Berkeley and Drummond," *Studies in English by Members of the University College Toronto* (Toronto, 1931), p. 184. Mr. Brett's main thesis had been anticipated by George Spencer Bowers, "The Philosophical Element in Shelley," *The Journal of*

Speculative Philosophy, XIV (1880), 446. But Bowers had never read the *Academical Questions*.

5. Mr. Brett's main thesis has been repeated by nearly all subsequent authors who have discussed Shelley's philosophy. Hans Liedtke, *Shelley—durch Berkeley und Drummond beinflusst?* (Greifswald, 1933), attempts no modification of Mr. Brett's hypothesis. But for some consideration of the anti-religious element in Drummond, overlooked by previous critics, see Kenneth Neill Cameron, *The Young Shelley: Genesis of a Radical* (New York, 1950), p. 393.

6. W. R. Sorley, *A History of English Philosophy* (New York, 1921), p. 276.

7. *The Works of Thomas Reid,* ed. Sir William Hamilton (Edinburgh, 1863), I, 108-110.

8. The painting now hangs in Marishal College, Aberdeen.

9. (London, 1811), pp. 177-178.

10. The reviewer was Francis Jeffrey: see his *Contributions to the Edinburgh Review* (London, 1844), III, 351-364.

11. Drummond's use of these terms in *Academical Questions* may be inferred from his footnote (p. xiv) explaining that he "generally understood the word *idea* in the same sense with most other modern philosophers."

12. For Shelley's reading of Cicero and rereading of Hume, see his letter to Thomas Jefferson Hogg, November 26, 1813. That he reread Drummond's *Academical Questions* may be inferred from the considerable influence that this book had on him after 1813 as well as from his letter to William Laing, dated September 27, 1815. For his reading of Diogenes Laertius, Sir Thomas Browne, and Montaigne, see *Mary Shelley's Journal,* ed. Frederick L. Jones (Norman, 1947), pp. 33, 40, 68.

NOTES TO CHAPTER IV

1. *Shelley* (New York, 1940), II, 135.

2. *The Pursuit of Death: A Study of Shelley's Poetry* (New York, 1933), p. 281.

3. "The Meaning of Mont Blanc," *PMLA*, LXII (1947), 1046-1047, 1051.

4. Amiykumar Sen, *Studies in Shelley* (Calcutta, 1936), p. 105.

5. See Frederick L. Jones, "Hogg and *The Necessity of Atheism*," *PMLA*, LII (1937), 423-426.

6. *Essays*, II, 17, note.

7. Southey's letter is given in White, *Shelley*, I, 618-620.

8. See Cameron, *The Young Shelley*, pp. 53-82.

9. *The Works of William Paley* (Philadelphia, n.d.), pp. 472-479.

10. *The Collected Works of Dugald Stewart*, ed. Sir William Hamilton (Edinburgh, 1854), VIII, 65, 85, 187.

11. *Enquiry Concerning Political Justice and Its Influence on Morals and Happiness*, ed. F. E. L. Priestly (Toronto, 1946), I, 80, 88, 91-92.

12. *Thoughts Occasioned by the Perusal of Dr. Parr's Spital Sermon* (London, 1801), p. 11.

13. *Essay on Sepluchres* (London, 1809), pp. 5-6.

14. *Shelley Memorials*, ed. Lady Jane Shelley (London, 1859), pp. 45-46.

15. Cf. Cameron, *The Young Shelley*, 194 ff.

16. *Thoughts on Man* (London, 1831), pp. 389-395.

17. The final line of *Hymn to Intellectual Beauty*. Elizabeth Nitchie, "Shelley's 'Hymn to Intellectual Beauty,'" *PMLA*, LXIII (1948), 753, points out that Shelley here uses the phrase "fear himself" in a favorable sense, that is, he uses the word "fear" in "its older sense of *revere* or *esteem*."

18. See Thomas Jefferson Hogg, "The Life of Percy Bysshe Shelley," in Wolfe (ed.), *The Life of Shelley*, I, 71.

19. See my "Shelley and Malthus," *PMLA*, LXVII (1952), 120 ff.

20. *Ideas and Men: The Story of Western Thought* (New York, 1950), pp. 325-326.

21. "Shelley, Godwin, Hume, and the Doctrine of Necessity," *SP*, XXXVII (1940), 638-639.

22. Mr. Kapstein (*PMLA*, LXII, 1055) holds that "awful doubt" refers to "doubt of nature's good intentions towards mankind." But Shelley would hardly have described such doubt as "awful"; nor would he have treated it as a reasonable alternative to "faith so mild."

23. William Michael Rossetti, *The Complete Poetical Works of Percy Bysshe Shelley* (London, 1894), III, 396, comments: "The meaning first suggested by the words 'but for such faith' is 'were it not for such faith.' The real meaning must however be 'only by means of such faith'.... A draft of the poem gives the phrase 'In such a faith' —which should, I humbly think, have been retained by the poet."

NOTES TO CHAPTER V

1. *The Life of Percy Bysshe Shelley* (London, 1886), I, 74-75.

2. *The Works of Walter Bagehot,* ed. Forrest Morgan (Hartford, 1891), I, 106.

3. "Platonism in Shelley," in *Essays and Studies by Members of the English Association* (Oxford, 1913), p. 98.

4. "Shelley," in *The Cambridge History of English Literature* (New York and Cambridge, 1916) XII, 74.

5. *Platonism* (Princeon, 1917), p. 284.

6. *The Magic Plant* (Chapel Hill, 1936), pp. 231, 432, *et passim.*

7. *Shelley's Religion* (Minneapolis, 1937), p. 287.

8. *The Platonism of Shelley: A Study of Platonism and the Poetic Mind* (Durham, 1949), p. 28.

9. Regarding the question of Shelley's knowledge of the Neoplatonists, see Notopoulos, *The Platonism of Shelley,* pp. 241-242, and Carl Grabo's review of this work in *MLN,* LXVII (1952), 57-61.

10. "Platonic Scholarship in Eighteenth-Century England," *MP,* XLI (1943), 103. Bolingbroke's phrase is quoted in Evans (p. 105).

11. All translations from Plato are from B. Jowett, *The Dialogues of Plato Translated into English with Analyses and Introductions,* 3rd ed. (Oxford, 1924).

12. Shelley's notes on the *Ion* are given in Notopoulos, *The Platonism of Shelley,* p. 485.

13. *Essayes,* II, 245.

14. See Chapter III, note 12.

15. See Edward John Trelawny, "The Recollections of Shelley and Byron," in Wolfe (ed.), *The Life of Shelley,* II, 199. Perhaps Shelley thought of Bacon as a sceptic because of his advocacy of the doctrine of the "two truths." For a study of Shelley and Bacon, see David Lee Clark, "Shelley and Bacon," *PMLA,* XLVIII (1933), 529-546.

16. For an account of Kant and his successors, see Frederick Mayer, *A History of Modern Philosophy* (New York, 1951), pp. 289-377.

17. As Mary Shelley remarked in her Note to *The Revolt of Islam,* Shelley had "two remarkable qualities of intellect—a brilliant imagination, and a logical exactness of reason." These two distinct qualities of his mind create in the poet a high degree of intellectual tension, which distinguishes his thought from that of the strict transcendentalist. Shelley was so opposed to any relaxation of the demands of reason to satisfy the imagination, that he took an unfavorable view of the

compromising empiricist: "Nor have those who are accustomed to profess the greatest veneration for the inductive system of Lord Bacon adhered with sufficient scrupulousness to its regulations" (VII, 63). Nor did the poet himself depart from such "scrupulousness," although he may seem to do so in his letter to Hogg, dated February, 1813: "Now do not tell me that Reason is a cold and insensible arbiter. Reason is only an assemblage of our better feelings—passion considered under a peculiar mode of its operation." Mr. Fairchild (*Religious Trends in English Poetry*, III, 354) has compared this remark with Wordsworth's definition of the imagination as "reason in her most exalted mood"; but this comparison is superficial and misleading. The real source of Shelley's remark is Hume, *Essays*, II, 161-162: "What is commonly, in a popular sense, called reason, and is so much recommended in moral discourses, is nothing but a general and a calm passion, which takes a comprehensive and distant view of its object, and actuates the will, without exciting any sensible emotion. A man, we say, is diligent in his profession from reason; that is, from a calm desire of riches and a fortune."

18. "Plato's Vision of the Ideas," *Mind*, XVII (1908), 505.

19. Cf. Sir David Ross, *Plato's Theory of Ideas* (Oxford, 1951), p. 21. Regarding the chronological order of Plato's dialogues, see Ross' table summarizing the views of five leading students on the subject (p. 2).

20. "Alastor: a Reinterpretation," *PMLA*, LXII (1947), 1024, 1026, 1038. Cf. Raymond D. Havens, "Shelley's 'Alastor,'" *PMLA*, XLV (1930), 1102-1103, and M. C. Wier, "Shelley's Alastor Again," *PMLA*, XLVI (1931), 950. Mr. Havens believes that "the reader of *Alastor* is confused because its author was confused" (p. 1108). Frederick L. Jones, "The Inconsistency of Shelley's Alastor," *ELH*, XIII (1946), 291-298, attributes this alleged confusion in *Alastor* to Shelley's failure to reconcile Wordsworth's mysticism with Locke's empiricism. For additional studies of the poem, see the following: Harold L. Hoffman, *An Odyssey of the Soul: Shelley's Alastor* (New York, 1933); Paul Mueschke and Earl Griggs, "Wordsworth as Prototype of the Poet in Shelley's 'Alastor,'" *PMLA*, XLIX (1934), 229-245; Arthur E. DuBois, "Alastor: the Spirit of Solitude," *JEGP*, XXXV (1936), 530-545.

21. Frederick L. Jones' view that "the *Hymn to Intellectual Beauty* is essentially a restatement of Wordsworth's *Ode: Intimations of Immortality*" ("On Life," *PMLA*, LXII, 777-778) overlooks the basic differences between the two poems and attaches too much importance

to remote parallels: cf. Elizabeth Nitchie, "Shelley's 'Hymn to Intellectual Beauty,'" *PMLA*, LXIII, 752.

22. *The Works of John Keats*, ed. H. Buxton Forman (New York, 1938-1939), II, 217. This parallel does not necessarily mean that Keats' poem influenced Shelley's, although Shelley was sufficiently familiar with Keats' *Endymion*. On the subject of Shelley's relation to Keats, see Carlos Baker and David Lee Clark, "Literary Sources of Shelley's 'The Witch of Atlas,'" *PMLA*, LVI (1941), 472-494.

23. For the autobiographical element in *Epipsychidion*, see White, *Shelley*, II, 255-269, and Kenneth Neill Cameron, "The Planet-Tempest Passage in *Epipsychidion*," *PMLA*, LXIII (1948), 950-972.

24. See Carlos Baker, *Shelley's Major Poetry: the Fabric of a Vision* (Princeton, 1948), pp. 266-267. Two main sources of *The Triumph of Life* are Petrarch's *Trionfi* and Dante's *Purgatorio*, XXVIII-XXXII: see A. C. Bradley, "Notes on Shelley's *Triumph of Life*," *MLR*, IX (1914), 441-456. M. F. Stawell, "Shelley's *Triumph of Life*," *Essays and Studies by Members of the English Association*, V (Oxford, 1914), 104-131, investigates Shelley's use of Goethe's *Faust*. William Cherubini, "Shelley's 'Own Symposium': *The Triumph of Life*," *SP*, XXXIX (1942), 559-570, interprets the poem as Shelley's first effort to deal with the "newly important problem of achieving communication with God."

NOTES TO CHAPTER VI

1. See Charles Kingsley, "Thoughts on Shelley and Byron," *Fraser's Magazine*, XLVIII (1853), 572; Solomon Francis Gingerich, *Essays in the Romantic Poets* (New York, 1924), pp. 195-239; Floyd Stovall, *Desire and Restraint in Shelley* (Durham, 1931), p. 217; Newman I. White, *The Best of Shelley* (New York, 1932), p. xl; Fairchild, *Religious Trends in English Poetry*, III, 28 ff.

2. See Bennett Weaver, *Toward the Understanding of Shelley* (Ann Arbor, 1932).

3. See Arthur C. Hicks, *The Place of Christianity in Shelley's Thought*. Unpublished Ph.D. thesis, Stanford University, 1932.

4. Edmund G. Gardner, "The Mysticism of Shelley," *Catholic World*, LXXXVIII (1908), 153.

5. Barnard, *Shelley's Religion*, p. 85.

6. *PMLA*, LXII, 782.

7. *Shelley*, I, 295-296.

8. *PMLA*, LXII, 781.

9. *The Chief Works of Spinoza*, trans. R. H. M. Elwes (New York, 1883), I, 6-7.

10. *The Complete Works of Thomas Paine*, ed. Philip S. Foner (New York, 1945), I, 464.

11. "Two Paths from Plato: Shelley and St. Augustine," *Catholic World*, CLIX (1944), 327.

12. *Religious Trends in English Poetry*, III, 341.

13. The *Essay on Christianity* has traditionally been assigned to the year 1815. Through a study of its relation to Shelley's reading as found in *Mary Shelley's Journal*, Mr. Notopoulos (*PMLA*, LVIII, 478-482) concludes that the *Essay* belongs to the latter part of 1816. More recently David Lee Clark—"Shelley's Biblical Extracts," *MLN*, LXVI (1951), 435-441—suggests that the *Essay* is an early draft of the lost *Biblical Extracts,* which Shelley composed and sent to Hookham in 1812. But the parallels that Mr. Clark notes between the thought and phraseology of the *Essay* and those of the letters and pamphlets of the period 1810-1813 do not appear to me to be conclusive, for he cites no evidence at all in support of his assertion that the thought and phraseology of the *Essay* are quite different from those of the period 1815-1820. It is my impression, as the present chapter suggests, that at least the ideas in the *Essay* are characteristic of the poet's mature thought.

14. Cf. Stovall, *Desire and Restraint in Shelley*, pp. 218-219.

15. *On the Poet Objective and Subjective; on the Latter's Aim; on Shelley as Man and Poet* (London, 1881), p. 15.

16. *The Best of Shelley*, p. xl.

17. *Shelley's Religion*, pp. 84-85, note.

NOTES TO CHAPTER VII

1. Cf. Kenneth Neill Cameron, "The Social Philosophy of Shelley," *Sewanee Review*, L (1942), 457-466.

2. Cf. Stephen C. Pepper, *The Basis of Criticism in the Arts* (Cambridge, 1946).

3. René Wellek and Austin Warren, *The Theory of Literature* (New York, 1949), p. 27.

INDEX

A NOTE ABOUT THE AUTHOR

CHRISTOS E. PULOS was born in Council Bluffs, Iowa, in 1909. He received his A.B. and M.A. degrees from the University of Nebraska in 1932 and 1933, and his Ph.D. from Iowa State University in 1947 after serving with the United States Army from 1942 to 1946. In 1947 he rejoined the faculty of the University of Nebraska where he is now Professor of English.

Dr. Pulos has contributed articles to *PMLA, Modern Language Notes,* and the *Journal of English and Germanic Philology,* and is the author of a study, *The New Critics and the Language of Poetry* (1958).